The Cut Flower SOURCEBOOK

EXCEPTIONAL PERENNIALS & WOODY PLANTS *for* CUTTING

The Cut Flower
SOURCEBOOK

EXCEPTIONAL PERENNIALS & WOODY PLANTS *for* CUTTING

Rachel Siegfried

With photographs by
Eva Nemeth

filbert *press*

To my granny, Barbara Lavers, for showing me that the garden is the best place to be.
Thank you to Ashley, my partner in life and in the garden, for your unrelenting hard work and support,
and for taking up the slack which has allowed me the time and space to write this book.

First published in 2023 by Filbert Press
filbertpress.com

Text © 2023 Rachel Siegfried

SPECIAL PHOTOGRAPHY Eva Nemeth
DESIGN Michael Whitehead

PICTURE CREDITS
Photographs by **Rachel Siegfried** except for the following by **Eva Nemeth**, front cover, 2, 5, 6, 8 btm, 10-11, 12,
14-15, 16-17, 18 btm, 19, 20 top left, 21, 23a and d, 24-5, 27 right, 28, 29, 30, 32-3, 34-5, 37, 38-9, 40-1, 42-3, 46
right, 47, 48-9, 52-3, 55, 58 top centre, 59 top left & centre, 60 top left, 60-1, 62, 64, 65, 66, 67, 70, 71, 72, 74-5,
76-7, 78-9, 80, 82 top, 83, 84 left & centre, 85, 86, 87, 88 left, 89, 90, 91, 93, 94, 96, 97, 98 centre & right, 99, 100,
101, 103, 104, 105, 108 centre, 109, 112-13, 115, 116-17, 120 left, 121, 122-3, 124-5, 127, 130 left & centre, 131,
140 top, 141 top, 142, 144, 145, 148 top, 159, 164-5, 167, 175 top left, 176, 212, 220, 225 top, 230 btm, 232-3,
236 top, 239, 240-1, 242-3, back cover; and **Fiona Hoare**, 31

A catalogue record for this book is available from the British Library

ISBN: 978-1-7399039-2-3

10 9 8 7 6 5 4   24 25 26 27 28 29 30

Printed in China

MIX
Paper | Supporting
responsible forestry
FSC
www.fsc.org FSC® C014688

Contents

Introduction

"I was first, and hope last to be, a gardener, it was an unanticipated combination of circumstances that led me to do professionally something I did once only as a relaxation, and much as I love doing it, I don't like the groove to be too deep." CONSTANCE SPRY, 1940

Chancing upon this quote by Constance Spry, I found it so relatable to my own experience. I too see myself primarily as a gardener with a love of plants and a deep connection to nature, so my floral style comes from that perspective. Working in the garden and walking my dogs in the surrounding countryside are my sources of inspiration and my design philosophy is simply about bringing some of the outside indoors.

My path to becoming a flower farmer and florist has been a meandering one, but there has always been a garden at the heart of it. The first was my granny's when I was child. It was her favourite place to be and it quickly became mine too, soothing and grounding me after my parents' separation.

Twenty years later, I had put my emotionally restorative experience of a garden into practice and become a garden designer for the NHS. It was while tending one of the gardens I had designed that I experienced the pleasure of picking a simple garden-gathered bunch and carefully wrapping it in newspaper. It was an encapsulation of the garden I had created and presenting it as a gift to a new love was surprisingly gratifying.

After a decade of designing gardens, I decided to move into productive horticulture and began work in a Victorian walled garden on a private estate in the Cotswolds. My job was to produce the vegetables, fruit and cut flowers for the 'big house'. Every Friday I would pick what was looking good in the beds and borders of the walled garden and the surrounding estate. Like Spry, I let my imagination run wild, bringing in artichoke heads from the kitchen garden to arrange with the old garden roses, and gathering handfuls of grasses and wild flowers from the meadows.

Gardening is at the heart of my approach to cut flowers. Here I am in my element with trowel in hand planting geum propagated from last year's trial bed.

I started to see everything as potential candidates for the vase. I would forage in the woods for brambles covered in juicy blackberries to complement the dahlias, and cut blossoming branches from the orchard to provide a framework for the tulips. The house had a cool flagstone-floored room lined with shelves of vases for flower arrangements. It became my flower laboratory where I experimented with the materials I brought in, learning about their vase life and how they worked in a display. I was mostly left to my own devices and given free rein to grow what I liked with no budget limits. I realize now how instrumental this self-education was; it changed the way I saw the garden and its plants. By cutting and arranging them, I was able to step even deeper into their sensory world – I could look at them in more detail, touch and smell them.

During the six years I spent growing cut flowers for the elite, I began to wonder why these garden-grown beauties were not more commonly available. It seemed strange that we had a slow food movement in the UK but not a floral equivalent. Surely enjoying flowers in your home should be a simple pleasure, without the environmental burden of air miles and chemicals? As a nation of gardeners, why were we so disconnected from the idea of buying flowers locally and seasonally, or even growing our own?

Determined to offer an alternative to sterile, imported blooms by providing flowers that would stop people in their tracks with their vital beauty, I left my job and, with my partner Ashley, took on an 0.8 hectare (2 acre) market garden. We settled on the name Green and Gorgeous and started clearing the cabbages to make way for my dream of a flower farm. My aim was to grow everything

Right: My whippet Jesse is a constant companion in the garden, here he has joined me to pick *Clematis tangutica* 'Golden Tiara' which has especially large, silky seedheads.

I needed to create border-to-vase arrangements guided by the seasons and the growth habit of the plants. I wanted to grow a palette of plants with intoxicating scent that would make grown women weep and leave an indelible memory of their fleeting beauty. To truly bring the garden in, I would explore all the stages of the plants' development, from the newness of freshly emerged spring growth to the muddy dishevelment of late autumn.

My belief in garden-grown cut flowers has been severely tested over the years. The vagaries of our weather, an army of pests, and high expectations from customers have certainly put my plant choices through their paces. I discovered that it was the perennials and shrubs I knew best from my work as a garden designer that met the practical challenges of growing for market. These stalwarts have also played a central role in developing my natural floral style as I moved from garden designer to flower farmer and florist.

Above: My morning commute to the flower farm is through the rusty gate just ten paces from our house. The more I learn about how plants work in a display the more it changes the way I think about the garden.

In my 'flower laboratory'
experimenting in late autumn
with supporting flowers and
foliage that work well with
chrysanthemums.

How the book works

In this book I am excited to share my low-impact approach to growing cut flowers, which centres around cultivating a backbone of permanent plants for cutting. My aim is to illustrate why perennials and woody cuts are such a natural fit for garden-inspired floral design by demonstrating their creative potential, practical benefits and light footprint on the environment.

Of course, knowing that they make sense is just the beginning. Then comes the fun bit of selecting which ones to grow. I am essentially a plant addict looking for an excuse to buy more, so it is with great pleasure that I will share my process of choosing and trialling plants. I will illustrate how I work back from the vase, sketching out in my mind what I need and allowing my plant knowledge to pick out the right palette of colours and forms to capture the seasonal moment. Your plant palette will not only be influenced by your own style and the purpose of your arrangements but also by the growing conditions you can offer. Perennials and shrubs are more of an initial investment than a packet of annual seeds, so right plant, right place is important. The next part of the book looks at the practicalities of laying out and preparing your plot; no matter the size, the principles are the same.

Below: The garden feels like the best place to arrange flowers. Here I can capture the floral moment with plants all around me to provide both materials and inspiration.

Above left: Newly divided bearded iris. This late summer task is repeated every three years to keep the plants at their most floriferous.

Above right: *Iris* 'Benton Susan' is one of the best of the Benton series bred by the late Sir Cedric Morris. I like their elegant form and muted colours.

Then, working through the seasons, I shall discuss the tasks related to growing these garden plants for cutting. The process is straightforward and will illustrate how little maintenance they require compared to annuals. To keep you inspired, each season will include a selection of what we are harvesting at that time so you can see how to achieve a continual flow of materials year-round.

As this is a sourcebook for growers of cut flowers I have dedicated a substantial part of it to the plant directory, which includes 128 main entries, the majority of which recommend more than one species or cultivar. These are all plants grown here on our farm, so I share my experience of growing and arranging with them and why they have made the cut.

Growing cut flowers, whether for pleasure or to make a living, has certainly flourished in the past decade. This book is aimed at being a useful reference for both the hobby and commercial cut-flower grower. If your ambitions are bigger than a small patch of ground there are tips on how to scale up in the chapter on Getting Started. For lists of plants that fulfil particular roles, turn to pages 20-21, 22-3, 58-60, 75, 83 and 87.

A Garden-led Philosophy

For a grower, the provenance of a cut flower is what makes it so special. I find this particularly true with the plants that come back year after year. Picking and arranging them is rather like having a good reminisce with an old friend. As you make an arrangement with what you have grown you reflect on the where and the when of each stem. In this way an arrangement can be a detailed and thoughtful composition to reflect upon, rather than purely a superficial decoration.

Seasonality

One of the best things about growing and picking flowers for a living is the deep connection it has given me with nature and its rhythms. Years of working outdoors have made me become finely tuned to the changing seasons. They govern my approach to flowers and I am grateful for the parameters they give me on what to pick and work with. The bewildering amount of choice available at a flower market or online would leave me floundering with indecision. Narrowing the decision-making down to what is looking at its best in the garden at that moment of harvesting is both reassuring and exhilarating. I feel that the spontaneity of taking my design cues from what is in season, rather than a disconnected client's brief, has helped me to become a more creative florist. Of course at some point I did have to make some decisions on what to plant, but it is a much slower, more considered approach to choosing and designing with flowers and in many ways is more akin to designing a planting scheme.

Climate change has started to blur the edges of our four distinct seasons and many of the plants I used to grow with great success have been struggling, particularly hardy annuals and spring-flowering bulbs. Perennials and woody cuts have proved their dependability in these challenging conditions, showing little variation in flowering times. This is quite an asset when you are growing cut flowers for a living and have orders to fulfil. Their reliability is coupled with how appropriate their peak flowering or fruiting times feel for the season they belong to – I like to think of it as nature's branding. Plants that flower at the same time tend to have an affinity with one another, complementing each other in the vase, which saves on the need for any 'over-arranging', the antithesis of natural-style floristry.

Roses are picked on the day they are to be arranged to get the most from their highly scented but fleeting beauty.

Right: In late winter, the first flowers I pick are hellebores. I can't resist a big handful, even though they will only last a couple of days. It is only when the flowers are pollinated and form seed pods that they become a viable cut flower.

Working in a garden every day, particularly a productive one, makes you appreciate that there are actually more than four seasons. The ancient Japanese were onto something when they developed 72 micro seasons, each just five days long. I love how they tune into the small changes of each broader season. After all, the first flush of spring in March is distinctly different to its maturity in May. For the purposes of this book I have divided each season into three to describe the ever-changing cycle and transience of flowers. My descriptions are not as poetic as the Japanese, simply 'early', 'mid' and 'late', and each is about four weeks or a month long. I refer to them when describing plants' flowering times in the

Above: *Paeonia* 'Claire de Lune' is the earliest peony to flower in late spring providing very welcome focal flowers during a lean time for this element.

Below: The autumn foliage of beech remains on the branch even when out of water. The leaves gradually turn from gold to tan as they dry. This longevity makes it a good base for wreath making.

plant directory and for seasonal tasks. These flower farming seasons are also illustrated in the Pick of the Garden pages, which show what there is to harvest throughout the year. I hope they demonstrate the sheer scope available for cutting within these seasonal plant groups and that there is always something to bring indoors.

EXTENDING AND BRIDGING THE SEASONS

Many of us do not have sufficient space, nor relaxed-enough neighbours, to erect a polytunnel in our gardens. Perennials and woody cuts offer an alternative way to stretch the season far beyond the six months that we can manage to grow annuals without protection in our climate. They are also brilliant for bridging gaps between the seasons.

Harvesting stems of early-flowering perennials such as geums and polemonium is very welcome after the spring-flowering bulbs have finished and hardy annuals are still in tight bud. Then by midsummer, when many hardy annuals have glutted and exhausted themselves, the choice of perennials reaches its peak. This bounty continues through to autumn as woody cuts come to the fore with their fiery foliage and fruit-laden branches. The winter is a pared-back affair of evergreens and catkins, but to me it feels seasonally appropriate. By early spring, perennial bulbs and the first flush of blossom are like a sigh of relief, weeks ahead of any annual plantings.

Left: Pussy willow is cut in late winter, before it flowers. The stems are stored in the barn, out of water, where they gradually dry and can be used for early spring arrangements.

EARLY-SPRING EXTENDERS

Cornus mas
Helleborus × hybridus
Hermodactylus tuberosus
Hyacinthoides hispanica
Narcissus
Ribes sanguineum
Spiraea thunbergii
Euphorbia amygdaloides var. *robbiae*
Lamprocapnos spectabilis (syn. *Dicentra spectabilis*)
Pulmonaria cultivars

SPRING TO SUMMER BRIDGERS

Allium hollandicum 'Purple Sensation'
Geum cultivars, eg Cocktail and Tempest series
Iris germanica
Lonicera × americana
Melica altissima 'Alba'
Paeonia hybrids and *P.* 'Claire de Lune'
Polemonium 'Lambrook Mauve'
Ranunculus acris 'Citrinus'
Tellima grandiflora
Stachys byzantina
Viburnum opulus

Hyacinthoides hispanica

Geum 'Bell Bank'

Narcissus 'Replete'

Lonicera × americana

AUTUMN EXTENDERS

Chrysanthemum (Incurved, Intermediate, Spider and Outdoor Spray types)
Chrysanthemum 'Avignon Pink'
Fagus sylvatica
Oryzopsis miliacea
Prunus spinosa
Rubus idaeus 'All Gold'
Symphyotrichum cordifolium 'Elegans'
Miscanthus sinensis (latest-flowering grass)

LATE-WINTER EXTENDERS

Alnus glutinosa
Galanthus 'Atkinsii'
Prunus cerasifera 'Pissardii'
Salix gracilistyla
Sarcococca hookeriana var. digyna

Chrysanthemum 'Avignon Pink'

Galanthus 'Atkinsii'

Miscanthus sinensis

Prunus cerasifera 'Pissardii'

Life cycles

If a plant can play more than one design role through the seasons it is worth considering, especially if you are growing cut flowers in a limited space. Using plants at different stages in their life cycle can make an arrangement feel more seasonally apt. It is refreshing to cut from them before or after their peak moment, perhaps for their foliage either side of their flowering season.

PERENNIALS FOR FOLIAGE

These are perennials I regularly use for their foliage, either before or after their flowering period.

BEFORE FLOWERING

Alchemilla mollis for its leaves and flowers in bud

Anthriscus sylvestris 'Raven's Wing' for its spring foliage

Arum italicum subsp. *italicum* 'Marmoratum' for its handsome marbled leaves

Alstroemeria cultivars for its flowers in bud

Cynara cardunculus for its architectural silver-grey jagged leaves

Epimedium sulphureum for its young bronze foliage

Foeniculum vulgare 'Purpureum' for its spring foliage

Macleaya microcarpa 'Spetchley Ruby' for its grey-green leaves produced on long petioles

Mentha cultivars for its many shades of fragrant green, silver and bronze foliage

Solidago rugosa 'Fireworks' for its acid-green buds before they open

Stachys byzantina for its foliage and buds before they open

Symphyotrichum 'Prairie Purple' for its dark stems and buds before they open

Thalictrum 'Elin' for its spring foliage

I particularly like using perennials that hold their structure after flowering. Some can be as beautiful in death as in life, meaning their picking season is extended from a matter of weeks to months. It is often the ones that are still standing by late winter that are the best. Many woody cuts also have this ability to change their appearance and play more than one role as a cut stem. If you choose to harvest from shrubs such as spiraea and viburnum in the spring and autumn you may well need to double up the number of plants, so that flowers are not sacrificed for fruits and vice versa.

AFTER FLOWERING

Amsonia hubrichtii for its autumn colour

Aruncus dioicus for its autumn colour

Crocosmia cultivars for their seedheads

Euphorbia schillingii for its autumn colour

Gillenia trifoliata for its autumn colour

Helleborus × hybridus for its flowers once they have gone to seed

Lysimachia clethroides for its autumn colour

Penstemon digitalis 'Husker Red' for its seedheads

Polemonium 'Lambrook Mauve' for its seedheads

Persicaria alpina for its seedheads

Opposite page, from left: *Alchemilla mollis, Alstroemeria* in bud, *Cynara cardunculus, Epimedium sulphureum*

Below, from left: *Mentha* cultivars, *Thalictrum* 'Elin', *Euphorbia schillingii, Helleborus × hybridus*

Growth habit

Capturing the essential character of a plant and translating it to the vase is much easier to do when you have watched it grow. Many of my observations come from my background in garden design, where I learnt about the habit of plants and how they interact with each other in a border. Without any formal training in floristry, I refer to this knowledge instead to guide me on how to position the stems in a vase. It is easier to emulate the natural growth habit of your flowers when you allow them a bit of space by using a vase with a generous, flared opening or by clustering vases together for a botanical look.

Right: Our cutting bed of bearded iris enjoys full sun and no competition from other plants which allows me to fully appreciate their unique form and array of colours en masse.

Below: To capture the simplicity of the border display above, here I have arranged the stems in a collection of ceramic bottles and vases made by the same potter for a unified effect.

Opposite: The open shape of a bowl allows flowers and foliage to be their natural selves. Everything included in this autumnal display strongly speaks of this moment in the garden. These are not stems that can be bought which makes the arrangement feel very personal and of this place. Included are the bronze-tinted *Lysimachia clethroides* and *Spiraea thunbergii* for foliage, *Anemone japonica* 'Whirlwind' as the focal flowers with 'All Gold' raspberries, *Crocosmia* seedheads and *Bouteloua gracilis* as textural accents.

Creating a distinctive look

One of the absolute joys of growing your own cut flowers is having the freedom to work with materials you would never be able to buy at a florist or flower market. It can feel immensely satisfying and empowering to know that you are able to create something that goes so much deeper than the standard shop-bought fare. Also, imported flowers are restricted by how well they transport and last out of water. Many are days or sometimes weeks old by the time they arrive in our shops. A lot of breeding has gone into making them so long-lasting, often at the expense of scent. In contrast, home-grown flowers can be fleeting, entrancing us with their vital beauty for just a few precious days. Often this ephemeral quality is combined with fragrance and a flood of memories and emotions. In my mind, the first inhalation of a rose is as special as seeing the first swallows arrive in spring. Another difference between shop-bought and home-grown flowers is stem length and the ramrod straightness of the former. It is seen as an asset, making the flowers easier to transport, process and throw together into formulaic bouquets. The opposite is sought after in garden-led floristry; kinky stems are treasured for the characterful shapes they make in a vase.

Perennials and woody cuts make it easy to create a distinctive look that is different not just from imported flowers but also annuals. The range of annuals for cutting is much wider than it used to be, but still doesn't come close to the almost limitless possibilities of these large plant groups. Each of us will choose our own unique blend of plants based on our style and growing conditions. It makes growing cut flowers endlessly interesting, as you will never run out of new plants to try and if you have customers they will appreciate seeing something unexpected in their bouquets.

Low-impact growing

For something that is not essential to our existence, it is shocking how much carbon and water are used to produce and import flowers. Their large footprint is combined with a good dose of pesticides and fungicides and finished off with plenty of single-use plastic to wrap and pack them for transportation.

Of course, many of us who grow cut flowers are already aware of how the floral industry is contributing to our deepening climate crisis. It may well be what motivated us to grow our own in the first place. In 2007 we set up Green and Gorgeous with the intention of offering local flowers with a low carbon footprint and a focus on seasonality. After witnessing the rise of the slow food

movement in this country I could see nothing comparable in the floral world, and was perplexed by the disconnect of a nation of garden-lovers unquestioningly buying their flowers from countries as far-flung as Kenya and Ecuador.

Initially, I focused on growing mostly annuals. They gave me the volume of flowers I needed to meet the demand and generate some income. We grew intensively on 0.8 hectare (2 acres) of land, making regular passes with the rotavator. After a few years the healthy abundance of what I call 'the honeymoon period' began to dwindle. Looking back at photographs of these bumper crops, I realized that I needed to slow things down and take a more considered approach to the soil to sustain flower production.

Above left: The kinky stems of honeysuckle are transformative, instantly bringing character and movement to a display. They can be used before and after flowering and by growing early and late flowering cultivars have a long picking period.

Above right: We wrap our flowers in paper for our customers to take home and also if they need to be stored. Here, peonies that were picked at marshmallow bud stage are held back from opening any further by being covered in damp newspaper and stored in our chiller out of water.

Right: *Digitalis purpurea* 'Camelot Lavender' is a short-lived perennial which can last for 2 years but we tend to grow it as an annual starting it fresh from seed each spring.

At the same time, the demand for our flowers had grown exponentially. We decided to take a new, low-impact approach and began a phased planting of perennials and woody plants in an adjacent 1.2 hectare (3 acre) field. It seemed like a good alternative to a minimum-till system for annuals on a large scale, where we would never be able to bring in enough material or manpower to keep mulching every year. Instead, we would cultivate flower crops that stay in the ground and protect the surface with their canopy, a living mulch. It would mean the soil's water retention would improve and carbon would be locked in rather than being released by continually working the soil. We would save on the fuel that this would have taken and keep our water bill down.

Below: Ash surveying the perennial field in late spring. Most of the heavy work was done earlier in the year.

The other reason for the move towards these backbone plants was the weather. After enduring extremes of it, including flooding and drought, the reality that we were experiencing climate change had hit home. I observed that it was the perennials that survived these challenging bouts of weather. It was their tolerance that kept the business afloat as annuals either collapsed in the sodden ground or quickly withered in the scorching heat.

Aside from needing the dependability that perennials and woody cuts could give the business, I wanted plants that are here year-round to offer protection and food to wildlife. We are surrounded by a desert of conventionally farmed arable fields and hedges flayed within an inch of their lives. Our biodiverse flower farm is a refuge in which I have witnessed a growing list of bird and insect species. This has made it an even more pleasurable place to spend my days. One of our biggest achievements is to have a growing population of swallows nesting in our farm gate shed – they bring as much joy to us and our customers as the flowers do.

Right: The aptly named Poppy, my right-hand florist, creating a dahlia bouquet at our Saturday farm gate.

Growing with natural ease

As growing a backbone of permanent plants for cutting is less work and risk in comparison to annuals, they consequently take less of a toll on the grower. As we become older and our acreage expands, these low-maintenance plants are the only way I can envisage our flower farming life continuing into retirement age. If you are cultivating cut flowers for pleasure, they should save you from becoming a slave to your cutting garden; if yours is a commercial enterprise, growing with natural ease will reduce the cost of production in terms of labour and inputs including fuel, water, compost and plastic.

Once you have made the initial investment of time and money to buy and establish the plants, most perennials and woody cuts need attention only once a year. Reassuringly, many are straightforward to propagate. As they are not repeatedly sown and grown, they use fewer resources; they do not require a stint in a heated greenhouse every year and less compost and fewer plastic pots are required for their production. They are mostly self-supporting and do not need staking, which reduces the amount of single-use plastic netting.

Division is the easiest and most economical way to propagate many perennials. This clump of astrantia is simply lifted, chopped up with a spade and replanted with just the addition of a spadeful of garden compost.

Peonies may have a short harvest window for a perennial but they make up for it with their longevity and hardiness as a plant. Here Ash and I are picking the highally scented, white cultivar 'Duchess of Nemours' for an imminent wedding so we select the blooms that are more open than the marshmallow bud stage.

For the risk-averse, perennials and shrubs are a good fit. They have a longer harvest period than annuals, which tend to glut, especially during a warm spell, when they can come and go in a fortnight. This waste is disappointing after all the effort invested in nurturing them from seeds. Some perennials will flush again if cut back and there are woody cuts which can have three stages of harvest. If all else fails and you have missed the opportunity to pick something, you have the reassurance of knowing there is always next year.

CHAPTER TWO

From Garden to Vase

If the design of your arrangements begins when you select what to grow, how do you go about making the right plant choices? With what appears to be an almost limitless range in these plant groups, it is a good idea to have some guidelines to help narrow down the selection.

Growing conditions

The garden's microclimate and site conditions have a direct correlation with what will end up in the vase. It is the starting point to choosing what I call the palette of plants for cutting. I have learnt the hard way not to let my desire for a plant override my knowledge of the farm's soil type, aspect and annual rainfall. The goal is to find plants that don't just manage, but thrive in these conditions. This is particularly relevant to the permanent plant groups discussed in this book, which need to have enough strength after being harvested regularly to come back with vigour the following year.

Signature style

Developing your unique floral style does not happen overnight and it is of course initially governed by the materials you have to work with. It will evolve gradually in tandem with your growing. As you gain a deeper understanding of what you like to put together, you will seek out plants that fit and over time build your palette of plants.

My arrangements were purely made up of flowers at first, then as the shrubs I had planted matured I moved towards a wilder, more informal style. The garden took off, becoming more abundant, and so did my vases, overflowing with variety. By this point I had all the materials to play with and explored every combination of colour and form to find what felt right. Once you reach this stage it is so much easier to find the plants that enhance your style and it is certainly one of the most enjoyable parts of growing your own materials for arranging.

Planning what to grow is usually a winter task, but it is also useful to make a note of gaps during the growing season. Sometimes I will just pick one stem of everything in flower to look at the bigger picture and note any gaps in an element (see pp 38-9), colour or form.

Balance and continuity

Once you understand your site and microclimate and are on your way to developing your unique style, the next thing to tackle is closing any gaps in the continuity of flowers and foliage. This is more complex than it sounds, as you are trying to achieve a seamless supply of all the elements of an arrangement – framework, focal, supporting and accent – so that you can have a good balance of materials to hand. Each season has a propensity to have more of one of the elements than the others, for example spring has plenty of focal flowers with all the flowering bulbs but the supporting element is thinner on the ground. The trick is to pay particular attention to these leaner times when planning your planting. Perennials and particularly woody cuts are expensive, especially when you need larger quantities for cutting, so unless you are certain that a plant is the right choice it is a good idea to trial it first in smaller amounts and then if possible propagate from it to increase the numbers. Most perennials are relatively easy to propagate either from seed, division or cuttings. For detailed advice, I recommend *The Propagation of Hardy Perennials* by Richard Bird.

Below, left: Mid- to late summer can be a gap time for focal flowers, as the roses finish and we wait for the dahlias to hit their flowering stride. Here, as an eyecatching alternative is *Echinacea pallida* with dramatic, swept-back petals and a bold central cone.

Below, right: Autumn is when foliage is at its most abundant and the opportunity to go big is hard to resist. I included four woody cuts in this large urn – beech, elder, snowberry and eucalyptus. Each has a purpose and combined they are almost enough without the addition of flowers.

Far left: A vintage silver, footed bowl found at my local bric-a-brac shop is the perfect shape for tumbling hellebore and honeysuckle stems.

Left: A glimpse of my rather large vase collection, which includes glass, metal and ceramic vessels in a variety of shapes and sizes.

Below: I prepare my bowls by positioning a pin holder in the bottom and placing a ball of chicken wire on top, held in place with a cross of florist's tape.

Vase and purpose

Every arrangement starts with a vase. The style, size and position of it will help to guide you on what to grow and cut. The more you work with different vases and understand the mechanics of arranging, the more informed your selection of materials for them becomes.

To appreciate each stem's character in an arrangement, I prefer to use a vase that allows for plenty of space. I favour vessels with a wide, flared rim and even better a foot for a bit of lift to make the most of trailing and arching shapes. A narrow neck with a fuller base also works well, allowing the stems to go in at an angle and fall open. Avoid cylindrical, narrow vases which squash all the flowers together so that all you see is the tops of their heads. All their nuanced character and individuality will be lost and each arrangement will end up looking rather generic.

The elements of an arrangement

To create a garden-inspired arrangement rich in a variety of textures and shapes, it is helpful to think about the plant material as four distinct elements that make up the whole. If you aim to grow plants that fall into these categories throughout the year you will always have sufficient material to make a well-balanced arrangement that is an engaging reflection of your garden at that moment in time.

STEP 1: FRAMEWORK

I always begin an arrangement by setting out its overall shape and size. For this I look for larger, sturdy branches that speak of the time of year and how they have grown; my aim is to reflect their habit in the way they are positioned in the vase. This framework offers support, while creating space for the other materials and connecting them to the vase. I choose just one plant for this element, in this case one of my mainstays – hornbeam, *Carpinus betulus*.

STEP 2: SUPPORTING MATERIAL

The next stage is to start to fill the space between the framework branches and provide a backdrop for the focal flowers. This 'understorey' material has slightly shorter stems so that it can create cover and volume in the main body of the arrangement. Depending on the season, supporting material can be flower or

Right: Branches of flowering hornbeam, *Carpinus betulus* are positioned at different heights and angles to form a sturdy framework.

Far right: An understorey layer of supporting foliage (*Thalictrum delavayi* and *Rosa glauca*) fills in between the framework branches bringing another dimension of colour and texture.

foliage, or a bit of both; I use it to add layers of colour and texture that will echo the focal element. Here I used *Rosa glauca* for its grey-red foliage and stems to link in with the dahlias and also *Thalictrum delavayi* foliage for its fern-like texture.

STEP 3: THE FOCAL FLOWERS

These are the attention-seekers which draw the eye with their bold shape, colour or size. I consider their growth habit, positioning them in clusters and facing in different directions. They are the most difficult element to get right, but often the fact that they belong to the same season and place is a good starting point. I include two or three focal elements. For this arrangement I chose the strong spires with hollyhock-like flowers of × *Alcalthaea suffrutescens* 'Parkallee' to contrast with *Dahlia* 'Seniors Hope'.

STEP 4: THE FINAL ACCENT

The finishing touch feels as if I am making gestural brushstrokes, which add air and movement, to bring the arrangement to life. By choosing the right colours and textures I can link all the elements together. They tend to be wispy plants, with finer stems and more details, and I try to restrain myself at this stage as including too many can be confusing to the eye. Here I have used feathertop grass, *Pennisetum villosum*, as its creamy flowers link with the hollyhock while its habit adds a blurry sense of motion.

Far left: The bold shapes of the focal flowers *Dahlia* 'Seniors Hope' and × *Alcalthaea suffrutescens* 'Parkallee' ground and define the arrangement.

Left: Grasses provide the accent element and are always an effective material for introducing air and movement. Here I used *Pennisetum villosum*.

A late summer arrangement capturing the seasonal moment by using all the elements – framework, focal, supporting and accent plants.

Framework

The architecture of an arrangement that defines its scale, outline and overall shape, framework is the first element to go into the vase, setting the stage for the showier blooms. On a practical note, it acts as scaffolding, supporting the other materials and linking the display to its vessel. In the garden, it is normally what is planted first in a new design – the trees, large shrubs and hedges – shaping the space for the layers of smaller, detailed planting that comes next.

The majority of framework materials are what florists and growers call 'woodies', primarily harvested from deciduous trees and shrubs. Any woody plant with ornamental characteristics can be used, although I recommend varieties that are relatively fast-growing, tough and vigorous so you can start picking from them as soon as possible without killing them off.

The trees and shrubs listed in the plant directory are all grown here on the farm and have been selected for several reasons, including characterful stems, early

FRAMEWORK TIPS
- There are a few taller perennials that have enough presence and linear form to make viable framework material and in a much shorter timescale. They need to be sturdy, branching and with flowers that are not too attention-grabbing – *Galega officinalis* is a good example.
- The main function of framework branches is their interesting shape, so avoid harvesting ones that are ramrod straight.
- Don't be afraid to do what florists call 'a bit of editing'. If you want to enhance a fruiting branch, just trim away some of the leaves. If there are too many flowers on a stem and it looks heavy, you can thin them out.
- Aim to capture the character of the plant while allowing it to do its job as the base layer.

spring blossom, distinctive autumn leaves, fruiting, catkins and scent. The branches of many make impressive stand-alone arrangements, filling a large vase with ease for an abundant garden-to-vase display.

Throughout the year, there is always something structural to harvest. In the winter months, I forage for bare branches tasselled with catkins such as those borne by alder and hazel. In early spring it is time for some hedgerow blossom from cherry plum and blackthorn. Next come budding foliage branches – anything with interesting shapes that will create movement and space. The new leaves will unfurl into the most promising shades of green.

In mid-spring, I visit our orchard, where trees are only pruned when it is blossom time. By midsummer, many woodies have filled out, with flowers and leaves forming a softer outline that becomes more backdrop foliage than structural material. By late summer, fruiting branches I pick regularly include thornless raspberry and snowberry. Berries turn to larger fruits such as crab apple and sloe as autumn colour brings another dimension.

Opposite page: Freshly harvested tall stems of *Salix gracilistyla* ready for drying in the barn.

Far left: Using loppers to harvest apple blossom in the orchard, the aim being to find branches still in pink bud. Blossom has a fleeting vase life and will shed its confetti petals very quickly if picked when the flowers are open.

Left: A large jug simply arranged with branches of apple blossom captures the abundance of spring and allows it to be enjoyed indoors. The jug has a narrow neck to hold the stems upright and a heavy bottom to ensure it doesn't tip over.

The emerging golden leaves of
Physocarpus opulifolius 'Dart's Gold'
in mid spring, perfectly timed to act
as a framework plant for narcissus.
The leaves fade to green as they
mature, so spring is the best time
to harvest the branches.

Supporting

A supporting plant is often described as a 'filler' which seems a rather bland way of describing such a valuable group. It can be foliage or a flowering stem and is often small in flower or leaf with a branching habit. This element is the understorey layer, filling in between the framework, so it can be shorter in length, creating cover and volume in the main body of the arrangement. Its role is to provide a physical backdrop or foil for the focal flowers to nestle in.

The majority of perennials and woody cuts can be classed as supporting materials, some performing this role at more than one stage in their growing season. Early-flowering trees and shrubs are particularly good at this multi-tasking, including spiraeas, viburnums, amelanchiers and crab apples. Shrubs and perennials are adept at filling the gap in this essential supporting role at the beginning and end of the season when annuals are not in flower.

Opposite page: Midsummer is a peak time for supporting perennials which I've arranged here in a cluster of tall glass bottles to display their many forms and textures using *Althaea cannabina, Campanula takesimana, Digitalis parvifolia, Gaura lindheimeri* 'Summer Breeze', *Lysimachia ephemerum, Penstemon barbatus* 'Jingle Bells' and *Thalictrum delavayi* 'Album'.

Below left: *Gypsophila paniculata* 'Single White' is the quintessential supporting flower with its clouds of tiny flowers on fine branching stems. This single form is much more elegant than the better known double-flowered baby's-breath.

Below right: In mid spring, blossoming branches of crab apple provide the supporting stems for the Darwin Hybrid tulip, 'Blushing Impression'.

In spring we have plenty of focal flowers, with a large number of tulips and ranunculus, and at the other end of the growing season in autumn we have dahlias and chrysanthemums. These are leaner times for supporting materials which help to balance the show-off large blooms with their less eye-catching, smaller features. This dearth is avoided in early spring by the blossoming branches in our cutting hedge and orchard. The woodland borders produce the first of the supporting perennials, delicate and understated lungwort and

maturing hellebores, a muddy green as they go to seed. By late spring the range expands to geums, jacob's ladder, buttercups and black-leaved cow parsley. In the autumn, berried and fruiting branches of shrubs and trees are a seasonally apt accompaniment in both colour and scale. In contrast, from mid to late summer the tables are turned when the perennials are at peak production and supporting becomes the plentiful element.

The fine stems of many supporting flowers, like astrantia, can be time consuming to pick, especially on this scale. It is often a team effort and sharp-pointed snips are the best tool for fast and precise harvesting.

Focals

Focals are the main players that grab your attention with their bold shape, size or colour. These floral stars call the shots on what the other elements will be, so I often pick them first and let them guide me around the cutting beds to find what will support and enhance them best. They are always flowers, usually large ones. The focal plants in this book include a few bulbs such as some of the more frou-frou double narcissus, perennial divas such as bearded iris and peonies, roses and of course dahlia and chrysanthemum blooms. I find some spire-shapes like delphiniums can be strong enough to be a focal, as can larger daisy shapes such as echinacea, whose 'eye' or cone will capture the attention of the viewer.

In an arrangement, I often include two or three different focal flowers that are variable in shape or size but harmonious in colour. I use only a few stems of each in a mixed arrangement as including too many will look heavy and unnatural.

Below: *Narcissus* 'Peach Swirl' has large, very double flowers with egg yolk orange centres. It's a showstopper for mid spring.

The proportion of this element to the others is a good indicator of how many you should plan to grow for a balanced palette of plants.

Like supporting plants, focal supply has peaks and troughs. Once the bulbs have finished flowering in late spring I have to work hard on my plant selection to fill the gap before the peonies begin flowering. I have discovered that intermediate bearded iris and peony hybrids are almost a month earlier than other cultivars. In midsummer, after the roses have finished their first flush, there can be a gap of a couple of weeks before the dahlias get into their stride, but dahlias left in the ground over winter will be in flower a month before the ones planted early in the year.

Positioning these larger flowers can be the trickiest part of creating an effortless, just-picked look. Avoid spacing them too evenly throughout the design. Consider how they were growing and place them in groups, at varying heights and facing in different directions.

Centre: A selection of my favourite dahlias including 'Penhill Dark Monarch', 'Josudi Andromeda', 'Salmon Runner', Seniors Hope' and 'Wine Eyed Jill'. Their colours blend well together and by using a range of shapes and sizes they sit happily together in one of my hand thrown bowls.

Below right: Many of the early-flowering peonies in late spring are single flowers with peach and coral shades well represented in this group. On the left is *Paeonia* 'Coral Charm' and right *P.* 'Soft Salmon Saucer'.

FOCAL TIPS

- When there is a fleeting abundance of peonies or roses I will often throw caution to the wind and arrange them en masse without any additional materials, so that they can enjoy all the limelight.
- Dahlias can hold their own in a vase because of the huge range of variety in size and flower shape.
- Only a quarter to a third of our mixed arrangements are focal flowers, so they only need to take up that much space on our land, especially if they are repeat flowering.

I like to use several rose cultivars together in harmonious colours that hark back to the beds they were cut from. This arrangement includes *Rosa* 'Champagne Moment', R. 'Golden Celebration', R. 'Port Sunlight', R. 'Sally Holmes' and *R. glauca* for its foliage.

Accents

Accent materials add the finishing touch to an arrangement and are the last element to be worked into a design. They tend to have fine stems which can easily be woven in at the end. These are dancers, adding a sense of movement, bringing the whole display to life. Their stems are often delicate and detailed, so they benefit from having length to extend beyond the main body of flowers and foliage. Many have arched, curved or kinky stems which create characterful, asymmetrical shapes out of negative space or any flat areas within the arrangement. This is my favourite element to both grow and arrange, so it is easy to get carried away. I have learnt to restrain myself, as including too many can be confusing and tiring to the eye.

All the grasses are characterized as accents. Their wispy, transparent stems do not impose too heavily but just enliven your work with a light, feathery touch.

Climbers are another accent group, with their ability to ramble and trail beyond the confines of the vase. Smaller bulbs, including snakeshead and fox grape fritillary and bluebells, are valuable as an accent in spring, which is a sparse time of year for this element. Later in this season, early-flowering perennials such as bleeding hearts and tellima with its question-mark-shaped stems make a quizzical addition.

In mid to late summer, tall perennials with wiry, branching stems and small button-like flowers such as sanguisorba, succisella and *Scabiosa ochroleuca* do an excellent job of adding an airy, meadow lightness to more substantial flowers. By autumn I often rely on the bead-like seedheads of crocosmia, which at this pared-back stage are almost even better than when in flower. Once they have lost their petals, *Lysimachia ephemerum* and *Rudbeckia triloba* with their bobbly seedheads make good little punctuation marks.

Below: Honeysuckle scrambling out of the vase; its pink buds are somewhere in between the shades of the sweet pea and the ranunculus, which helps to bring them together.

The plant palette

Just as a painter works with a palette of paints to express their style and subject matter, so the flower-grower selects plants as their raw material to build their own unique palette of forms, colours and textures.

FORM

Plant choice is often based primarily on colour; it is often what we first notice about a flower and we all have our favourite shades. However, I would argue that the plants' forms and how their different shapes work together are more important. Often colour can be fleeting while the structure of the plant remains. This is particularly true of perennials, which have many stages of growth and consequently different shapes throughout the year. First there are the buds, then unfurling leaves, flowers followed by seedheads, autumn foliage and lastly the wintry skeletal remains.

When I am designing an arrangement I select a mix of forms to create contrast, for example the vertical energy of a spire counterbalanced by the soft horizontal lines of an umbel. I am also looking for shapes to help evoke a mood, style or sense of place. Umbels and daisy shapes belong in sun-warmed meadows and prairies, for example, while the bowl shapes of peonies, roses and waterlily dahlias feel decadent and luscious. Planning for continuity of form can be challenging but worth attempting to maintain a balanced plant palette through the seasons. I tend to work with harmonious colours, so enjoy working with a variety of forms that sit comfortably with each other colour wise. Among the most useful shapes are spires and spikes, which are plentiful in perennials from early to midsummer but harder to find after that. Instead, I seek out grasses with a similar form through late summer and autumn.

Below: The clusters of daisy-shaped *Rudbeckia triloba* evoke a prairie feel when they are combined with the bleached seedheads of grasses. They contrast boldly in form but are harmonious in colour.

Flower shapes

BELL-SHAPED PLANTS with arching stems of pendulous bells include campanula, clematis and fritillary.

BOWL- OR CUP-SHAPED Full-bodied flowers, often large and abundant with petals, such as peony, garden rose and dahlia.

BUTTONS AND GLOBES Concentrated clusters of flowers stand out like defined points against softer forms, such as echinops, eryngium, allium, agapanthus and astrantia.

Campanula takesimana

Paeonia 'Coral Charm'

Allium 'Mount Everest'

Clematis 'Twinkle'

Chrysanthemum 'Bigoudi Red'

Eryngium planum 'Blue Glitter'

DAISY-SHAPED I use this term to describe any flower with rays and a central eye, a sunny and optimistic shape prevalent in late summer and early autumn. Examples are aster, echinacea, Japanese anemone, rudbeckia.

PLUMES Myriad tiny, individual flowers arranged in a fluffy, relaxed manner which make them useful for linking more defined forms, for example artemisia, miscanthus, persicaria and solidago.

SCREENS 'Transparent' plants have a fine network of stems which allow you to see straight through them. They are useful for adding air and movement. Plants in this category include cow parsley, panicum, sanguisorba, stipa and thalictrum.

Echinacea purpurea 'White Swan'

Persicaria alpina

Anthriscus sylvestris 'Ravenswing'

Cephalaria gigantea

Aruncus dioicus 'Horatio'

Gillenia trifoliata

SPIRES AND SPIKES A dominant visual element, dramatic at scale or in large groups, they bring definition to loose, undefined forms. Examples are calamagrostis, delphinium, foxglove, lysimachia, salvia, verbascum and veronicastrum.

UMBELS Some are true members of the umbellifer family while others just share a similar upturned bowl shape, which can be dense or lacy. Examples include achillea, ageratina, foeniculum, phlox and sedum.

Delphinium elatum New Millennium Series

Achillea millefollium 'Summer Pastels'

Verbascum hybridum 'Southern Charm'

Chaerophyllum hirsutum 'Roseum'

Centre: A harmonious arrangement in shades of pink and red. To create contrast, I have used them in both muted and deep, intense shades, the blush pink of *Dahlia* 'Sweet Nathalie' and snowberry supporting the rich pop of the HOT CHOCOLATE rose and *Dahlia* 'Copperboy'.

Left: I am always looking for subtle connections in colour when selecting what to pick. By holding the flowering crab apple branch up to the tulip bed I pick out one variety whose blushing centre matches perfectly.

COLOUR

I tend not to teach colour theory in my floristry classes, as I am aware that appreciation of colour is a personal thing and there are no rights and wrongs when it comes to self-expression. All I will say is that it is easier to work with shades that are next to each other on the colour wheel. It results in an arrangement with a more cohesive and harmonious quality. Working within a colour theme also allows for a more detailed and nuanced approach, as it makes you look beyond the flowers to see how a bud, stem or even the detail of a leaf vein could potentially work together.

Perennials and woody cuts are great plants for this more considered way of looking at colour, for just as the plants change shape throughout the year so they also display a surprising amount of variation in their hue. They can be luminously tinted by the vigour and freshness of spring or shaded by the first cold nights of autumn. Many are far subtler in colour than annuals, as they have an earthy tone which prevents arrangements from becoming too sweet, keeping them grounded and garden-led.

All colours have their peak season, for instance true blue flowers are most abundant from spring to midsummer, after which they become increasingly scarce. If continuity of a favourite colour is important it will take time to figure out when the gaps are and what plant or which part of it might fill it. Of course there is a lot of fun to be had doing this and an ever-increasing plot size!

It is always worth growing plenty of neutrals, which I class as primarily shades of green in a range of warm and cool tones. These will come from a combination of woody cuts and perennials, which can be used before or after flowering. Any plants with leaves or flowers in silver, cream, beige, off-whites or shades of brown also qualify as neutrals and will work across many different colour themes.

TEXTURE
While texture has long been an underrated aspect of floral design, that is changing with the growing interest in seasonal flowers and foliage. The use of dried materials is back in fashion, but this time often alongside fresh, which demonstrates this awareness of texture and how contrast in it brings another layer of interest to an arrangement.

Perennials and woody cuts offer a series of textures as they emerge, flower and age, for example the pleats and crinkle cuts of young foliage on deciduous branches, the satiny sheen of rose petals as they open. Texture reaches its peak in autumn when you can make the most of it by contrasting hard, shiny fruits, fluffy grasses and crisp wind-blown leaves.

Above: Looking for something special at one of my favourite rare plant fairs. It is held in late spring when I am always on the hunt for plants to bridge the seasonal gap.

Sourcing

Plant shopping is one of the most enjoyable parts of being a flower farmer, and with acres to fill I always have an excuse to visit a plant fair or specialist nursery on one of my 'research' days. Gardens and other flower farms are also a good source of inspiration, as seeing the plants growing in the ground tells me a lot about how they might behave in a vase. These visits are so useful for filling the gaps in your palette. Try to get out and about at times of the year when there is a gap in flowering, such as the cusp of late spring into early summer.

Buying plants from fairs and nurseries is a lot more expensive than my usual trade purchases but it is so worthwhile to seek out these places and all their treasures if you want to create a difference in your work. I tend to buy only two or three of a potential contender as I am keen to trial plants before allowing them to occupy space and time on the farm.

Trialling

To understand if the plant you are hankering after would work well in your garden, it is a good idea to grow a small number first. We have beds for this purpose, dotted around the farm in different growing conditions. You will need to grow most perennials for a couple of years to get a true picture of their practicalities as a productive plant for cutting. Hopefully by then they will be large enough to propagate if they are a keeper.

When you are considering a new plant, it is a good idea to use a checklist of criteria to observe its potential:

HEALTH AND VIGOUR These are at the top of the list, since a plant has to be able to thrive in your growing conditions to produce enough material to cut from on a regular basis, particularly if you are hoping to use it commercially.

HEIGHT Does it reach a satisfactory eventual height? Often plants do not fulfil the heights promised on their description, perhaps because the conditions are not ideal. If a plant is less than 30cm (12in) it is probably too short to be used frequently enough.

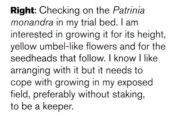

Right: Checking on the *Patrinia monandra* in my trial bed. I am interested in growing it for its height, yellow umbel-like flowers and for the seedheads that follow. I know I like arranging with it but it needs to cope with growing in my exposed field, preferably without staking, to be a keeper.

Opposite page: My first row of *Delphinium* New Millennium Series was grown from seed in 2010 and ticked all the boxes on my trial list. It has one drawback and that is keeping the towering spires upright. A sheltered position, strong netting positioned fairly high and not too much fertility to keep the stems sturdy has worked well.

SPACE Can you work out how much space it will need when planted in quantity? I tend to plant most perennials at 30–50cm (12–20in) apart and see how quickly they create a closed canopy.

YIELD How many stems can you harvest in its second year? Does it have different stages of harvest?

ELEMENT How can it be used in a design, which element is it (see pp 38-9) and will it help to develop a more balanced mix of materials in your garden?

COLOUR Will it contribute to your floral style and palette? I like to work with different tones of the same colour, so I look for plants that flower at the same time in a similar hue.

VASE LIFE How long does the flower last in the vase? Ideally, I want about five days from a stem to consider it vase-worthy.

Below: *Geum* 'Mai Tai' plants are spaced 30cm (12 in) apart in a triple row. This fills a metre- (yard-) wide bed and in a year's time there will be no bare soil for weeds to colonize.

BULKING UP

If a perennial is a keeper, the next step is to bulk it up, so that it can be block planted in beds that are a metre (yard) wide for efficient harvesting. To make a sufficient block requires at least 20 plants. I use propagation methods which will yield as much as possible from my trial plant – namely summer micro-division for early perennials and grasses and basal cuttings for later-flowering perennials.

Above: After trialling *Geum* 'Mai Tai' I decided to forgive its slightly short stature because its colouring is exquisite with peach-pink flowers enhanced by deep maroon stems. Here, the stem colour is set off by *Anthriscus* 'Raven's Wing' and Japanese painted fern leaves. To stop it feeling too sombre I added the lightening touch of *Melica altissima* 'Alba'.

CHAPTER THREE

Getting Started

It is easy to be tempted just to slot plants for cutting into existing borders in your garden or design a perennial cut flower border, which is really a herbaceous border in disguise. I fell into the latter trap when I first started Green and Gorgeous. It was painful to transition from a characterful walled garden to a field of cabbages and a polytunnel, and to help me acclimatize I immediately set about planting two central borders in such a way. However, I barely cut from them as I don't want to ruin the show and they take more time to maintain than all the more efficient and productive beds. With this in mind, it is a good idea to design and maintain the cutting area separately from the rest of your garden, no matter its size.

Planning

It is all too easy to get carried away with what you want to grow rather than focusing on what you are actually able to grow. Understanding your site is the first step to planning your bed layout and planting. Soil type, drainage, aspect, exposure, frost pockets and perennial weeds will all have an influence. As your backbone plants are in it for the long haul, it is important to take your time getting them right.

Below left: Our central borders are at their best in late spring with drifts of alliums and sweet rocket. It is difficult to pick from a mixed planting such as this on both a practical and aesthetic level.

Below: The perennial field is laid out in crop-like blocks and rows which still have a strong visual impact but are also straightforward to harvest and maintain.

SOIL

Before taking on the land at Green and Gorgeous I spent a day working on the site. It was originally an organic market garden, so I was tasked with harvesting vegetables. The reason I was there was to assess the soil and after a morning of digging leeks I had a pretty good idea of it – a beautiful silty loam, rich and almost stone-free. After working on poor Cotswold brash for the previous six years it was almost enough to make me sign on the dotted line there and then.

Soil can be improved by applying lots of organic matter, but you cannot fundamentally change it, so it helps to know what you are working with. We take regular soil tests in different parts of the farm and send them off to a soil analysis lab for a small fee. The results enlighten us on what trace minerals are lacking and what we need to add to improve the soil for planting. Plants that enjoy a rich soil are mulched annually with our own garden compost, which is primarily made from shredded garden clippings and well-rotted horse manure.

ASPECT

The majority of our perennials and shrubs are planted in an open, sunny position. All the rows are orientated north to south, so that they can make the most of the light rather than be shaded out by their neighbours. The east side of our field is edged by a row of mature horse chestnut trees; the phlox, geum and astrantia appreciate the shade cast from them in the mornings. Unlike annuals, there are many perennials that appreciate partial shade, so it should be valued, or even actively encouraged, as it will widen the scope of what you can grow.

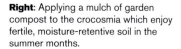

Right: Applying a mulch of garden compost to the crocosmia which enjoy fertile, moisture-retentive soil in the summer months.

BED SHAPE

Rectangular beds are the most efficient and productive shape for growing cut flowers. It is easier to calculate how many plants you need, space them evenly, then weed, irrigate and support them. The beds can be as long as you like, but should be no more than 1.2m (4ft) wide, so that you can reach plants in the middle without stepping on the bed. As our beds are 50m (164ft) long they are just 1m (3¼ft) in width since the length means I have to be able to step over them easily without doing the splits!

PATHS

There are two things to consider with paths: their width and how to control the weeds. If aesthetics are important then mown grass, straw or bark chippings will be contenders, but they all need regular maintenance. We have two kinds of path. The wider ones are for moving around the farm either on foot or by machinery, and as we are open to the public aesthetics are important to us, so these are grass, which looks good. They do need regular mowing, of course, so think about the width of your mower when designing their dimensions. For the paths between the cutting beds we favour a thick grade of landscape fabric (100g per sq m/3oz per sq yd), held down firmly with pegs. For the majority of perennials and grasses a 50cm (20in) width suffices and for most woody cuts 1m (3¼ft). Once a year, after the big cut-back in late winter, all it needs is a scrape with a hoe and a sweep with a stiff brush to keep any soil and weed seeds from settling on it. The entire perimeter of the plot is also edged in 1m (3¼ft) wide landscape fabric to stop grass creeping in from the sides, which it will do surprisingly quickly.

Above: The grass paths around the perimeter of the field are wide enough to accommodate the tractor. This is useful for bringing in loads of compost for mulching and gives the flower farm more of a garden feel.

MULCHING AND WEEDS

It is essential to get rid of any perennial weeds before you start planting. For a few years, we grew just annuals in some beds, attacking the weeds each time a crop was cleared. As most perennials and grasses are clump-forming they will spread and form a closed canopy, smothering out any new annual weed competition. Some do this remarkably quickly, especially when they are planted closely together. Our spacing is much tighter than gardening catalogues advise. I have never found this to be a problem as the plants are harvested regularly, which keeps them in check. Originally we planted through burnt holes in landscape fabric, but this is only really effective with perennials that are slow-growing or do not have a spreading habit. You also run the risk of creating the perfect habitat for rodents, which will enjoy its shelter while consuming the roots of your plants.

WATER

Perennials and woody cuts are generally more tolerant of water shortages than annuals, especially once they are established. However, if they have experienced a period of drought their stems will be shorter and the quality and number of flowers will be reduced. As the climate is changing many of us are experiencing prolonged periods of dry weather, so to ensure good stem length and an abundant, healthy harvest there are key times of the year when consistent watering is essential. These are in mid-spring, when the main surge of growth occurs, and also when flowering stems and buds are forming.

It is a good idea to have a simple irrigation system in place. To be economical with water and get it directly to the roots of the plant, a drip tape system is cheap, effective, and easy to install, fix and alter over the season. It can also be used to run liquid feed through via a diluter. The tape does require linear-shaped beds, the longer the better, to save on connections and fittings. Drip irrigation is designed to work on low pressures and can cover large areas. A line of tape will water an area approximately 30cm (12in) wide, so we use three lines on our 1m (3¼ft) wide beds. They are pegged in position or woven through the plants to keep the tapes in place.

SHELTER

If your cutting beds are situated in an exposed position they could potentially suffer damage from prevailing winds and freezing temperatures. One of your first jobs will be to establish the direction of the most damaging winds and plan a shelter belt of fast-growing woody cuts to protect your planting. This is the opportunity for a cutting hedge full of foliage and both flowering and fruiting

Left: Newly planted achillea are helped to establish during a very dry spring with three lines of drip tape irrigation.

Right: The original field is protected by an old 4-metre (13-ft) hawthorn hedge. The temperature is noticeably warmer here than in the open field reminding me of my days working in a walled garden.

Below: The miscanthus hedge stands well all winter, so despite being herbaceous it offers protection from midsummer through to early spring.

branches. Look for trees and shrubs that are tough and fast-growing. They also need to be affordable if you are planting a large area. Bare-root hedging plants are a good option; if they are to be planted as a double staggered hedge make sure you can access both sides, but if this is not possible a single row will suffice. Initially it might be necessary to put up an artificial windbreak until your living one has established. We use plastic mesh, but for a garden setting woven hazel hurdles look good and are effective. As a rule, the windbreak protection extends to a cropping distance of ten times the height of your hedge, so 2.5m (8 ¼ft) will protect 25m (82ft) of planting. If you are only concerned about south westerlies in the summer months it might be worth considering tall perennials and grasses as a windbreak; my miscanthus hedge has done a sterling job at filtering the wind, to the extent that I have not had to stake plants on the leeward side since it has become established.

CUTTING HEDGE

The majority of plants used for a cutting hedge are deciduous trees and shrubs. They are chosen for their ability to cope with exposure to cold, drying winds, relatively fast growth and low price when bought in large numbers.

Alnus cordata
Betula pendula
Carpinus betulus
Corylus avellana
Crataegus monogyna
Eucalyptus gunnii
Eucalyptus parvula
Euonymus europaeus
Fagus sylvatica

Malus sylvestris
Physocarpus opulifolius
Prunus cerasifera
Prunus spinosa
Rosa glauca
Salix gracilistyla
Syringa vulgaris
Viburnum opulus

Above, from left: The fast-growing *Eucalyptus gunnii* can reach 4m (13ft) by its second year. Blackthorn puts on a lot of growth rapidly providing an abundance of early blossoming branches while also providing a rough shelter belt. *Viburnum opulus* is covered in creamy green lacecap flowers in late spring.

Right: Harvesting pussy willow, which is coppiced every two to three years for taller stems and so that it continues to provide a windbreak through the summer months.

Right: My three most used hand tools which normally have a band of red tape around the handles to prevent them ending up in the compost heap. From left to right: bamboo hand rake, flower snips, razor hoe.

Right: The springy tines of the bamboo rake remove cut-back material with a lightness of touch and it is small enough to get in among the plants.

Far right: Making a sharp, clean cut is important for the vase life of the stem and for the health of the plant. With snips I can get right in above a node which means no die back and encourages more flowers if it is a cut-and-come-again plant.

Favourite hand tools

Using the right tools will make the performing of tasks more efficient and less tiring. Whether I am planting, weeding or harvesting, all of my favourite tools seem to be Japanese, which I appreciate for their precision and quality.

BAMBOO HAND RAKE

This tool is like a giant springy helping hand for gathering up all the cut-back debris. Made from split bamboo, the clawed tines are lightweight and strong.

FLOWER SNIPS

I don't wear a holster, so I need snips that are small and lightweight, comfortably fitting in my back pocket without doing any harm. The pointed ends allow me to get right into dense plantings and cut with precision. They are also essential for my floristry work, so they virtually live in my hand all summer.

RAZOR HOE

For weeding, nothing beats this short-handled hoe. Its sharp-pointed blade can get into tight spots between close planting and it is supremely comfortable to use.

Getting mechanized

When you scale up to field-grown plants, it's time to put the hand tools and barrows to one side and get mechanized. We grow our cut flowers on 2 hectares (5 acres) of land, which would be a herculean task to manage entirely by hand. As the flower farm grew, so did our machinery. It was our way of avoiding exhaustion and keeping labour costs down.

For garden machines to work efficiently, your site will need to be designed to accommodate them. Our perennial beds have been set up to enable the tractor to drive over them with its tyres on the adjoining paths. There is plenty of space at either end of the rows for turning vehicles, and down one side for composting and storing mulching material.

In late winter, Ashley drives the tractor up and down the perennial rows with a flail mower, cutting all the dead top growth back to the ground. It is a satisfyingly quick job which only takes one person. As the flail cuts it also shreds, so we can leave everything on the beds as a mulch. If you are on good soil and want to grow your perennials hard so that the taller varieties do not require staking, this is probably all the plants will need.

Not all of us have the set-up for a tractor and there are many beds in our garden that need something a bit smaller. The hedge trimmer is a valuable tool for cutting back swathes of woody material at the beginning of the season. Subsequent cuts in the summer months encourage a second flush of flowers.

Above: In the field our paths have been laid out to the same width as the distance between the tractor tyres so that Ash can drive over the beds for topping and mulching in late winter.

Right: The hedgecutter is great for woody stems like this hypericum, especially when you are growing them en masse and need to save time and avoid repetitive strain injury.

SHREDDING

All the woody material generated from cutting back and clearing would be too much for the compost heap, turning it dry and dormant. We use a shredder to break it down into small pieces which help activate the rotting process.

MULCHING MATTERS

If you are growing field scale, a tractor with a transport box will make moving a few tonnes of mulch a less daunting prospect. The box is reversed into a mound of mulch, scooping up barrow loads at a time. It is then driven down the rows with two people behind, spreading it on to the beds.

HARVESTING

Ideally, flowers should be picked into buckets of water and then transported back to a cool space as swiftly as possible to take out any field heat. As our acreage grew, this became an increasingly epic task, so we purchased a second-hand utility vehicle on eBay. We call it our 'picking buggy'. Out of harvesting season, it doubles up as a hauler of compost, plants, tools and basically anything that saves me and the team having to carry or barrow.

Above, left: A dung fork is a good, lightweight tool for shifting mulching material off the transport box and onto the rows quickly and lightly.

Above, right: The picking buggy in a shady spot under a damson tree. It can take twelve buckets at a time which saves a lot of leg work and heavy carrying.

Spring tasks

As in most gardens, spring is the busiest time of year on our flower farm. There are hundreds of plants to propagate by seed, cuttings or division and the race is on to have flowers to harvest from them later in the season. The frenetic pace of spring tasks steps up a notch as the autumn-planted bulbs begin to flower and the balancing act of growing and harvesting begins.

Above: Spring is my favourite season for creating bowl arrangements. Their open shape means I can make the most of all the focal flowers provided by the autumn-planted bulbs.

Right: *Narcissus recurvus* with its elegant reflexed petals is the last narcissus to flower in late spring. Here it enjoys the dappled shade of our woodland border where inspiration for an arrangement comes from planting companions melica grass and solomon's seal.

Right: Sowing the saved seed of scabious in a half-sized seed tray, which will yield about fifty plants. If you don't have a greenhouse or bottom heat, you could sow late summer to early autumn in a sheltered place outdoors.

Below: *Achillea* 'Summer Pastels' flowering in its first year in late summer from an early spring sowing.

SEED-SOWING

Raising perennials from seed is by far the cheapest way to produce a multitude of plants when you are attempting to create a row or block of a species. It is also surprisingly easy, especially if the seed is fresh. Straight species or seed-raised selections are the ones to seek out, either from a reputable supplier or from freshly saved seed. We choose to sow the majority of the perennials grown from seed in spring, with the exception of seeds that need cold stratification, in other words a few frosts, to break any germination inhibitors. To work out which those are I recommend a good read of the Jelitto Perennial Seeds catalogue, which includes detailed sowing guidelines for each species. If you have missed the autumn sowing window or are impatient, like me, have a look at their Gold Nugget Seed range, which has been treated to eliminate their natural dormancy.

First-year-flowering perennials

The first-year-flowering perennials are sown as soon as the heat mat gets switched on in late winter. By starting these right at the beginning of the season, my aim is to time their flowering for mid to late summer in the same year. They all tend to be supporting flowers, which are very welcome at this time when many of the annuals have run out of steam. The plant will adjust back to its normal flowering period in early summer the following year. I sow some plants annually so I have a couple of patches, with first- and second-year sowings flowering successively.

Sowing kit

There is no magic art to successful germination – it is just down to having the optimum conditions. If you are very keen, or growing for a living, then it is worth investing in a heat mat so you can provide bottom heat. It will increase the success and speed of germination, meaning you can move trays on quickly and get another batch going. A grow light is a worthwhile investment too, especially if you are not using a greenhouse or you start sowing in late winter. Watering at this delicate stage is best undertaken by placing trays in a shallow water bath to let them imbibe gradually; it is less risky than overhead watering and easier to achieve even moisture.

The main reason for germination failure is that seeds have dried out. Covering them with a layer of fine vermiculite or grit allows a thin film of moisture to be held around the seeds. It keeps them warm, allows in light and because it is sterile they are less likely to succumb to fungal diseases and damping off.

Above, left: A light dusting of fine vermiculite is all most seeds get, about twice the depth of the seed is a good rule of thumb.

Above, right: I can fit fifteen half-sized seed trays (each 22 x 16 x 5cm or 8½ x 6 x 2in) under the growlight which needs to be quite close to the seedlings to stop them from getting drawn.

Early spring slowly creeps out of the monochrome of winter. Small signs that change is afoot appear in our cutting hedge. A froth of delicate blush and ivory blossom flushes on the cherry plum and blackthorn. In the orchard there follows a succession of plum, damson and pear. Bare flowering branches are having their moment, ribes and forsythia picked in bud and forced into flower indoors. I cut long branches, appreciating their scale and simplicity.

The eucalyptus season is coming to an end, as the spring equinox marks its time to be pollarded for another year. We pick every stem, using their glaucous silver and olive colouring as a backdrop for the custard creams and peaches of the first narcissi. Their fragrance and cheery colour can convince you its spring even if the weather is not obliging. The more discreet and mysterious widow iris stand in a small bowl on my desk where they can be studied in all of their exquisite detail. If they remained outdoors I know that in the rush of spring tasks their flowering would be overlooked. Shimmering pussy willow buds suspended by drying hold their metallic sheen and hellebores become more reliable as cut flowers now their seed pods have started to swell. The choice is limited this early in the season but the flowers are more deeply appreciated for it.

Narcissus 'Pink Dawn' flowering in our yard troughs, where I like to trial varieties before lifting them after flowering to transplant into cutting beds for next year.

The white flowers of *Ribes* 'Elkington White' time their opening perfectly between the first flush of cherry plum and blackthorn blossom in the hedgerow to the relay of flowering branches in the orchard.

In early spring, what to pick and bring indoors is limited so I tend to do simple single genus arrangements and group them together. Hellebores and branches of cherry plum blossom work well together.

Right: The deeper tray means the plug plants are less likely to dry out and it buys a bit of time if the ground is not yet ready for planting.

Far right: The greenhouse staging is designed to take a double row of our modular trays so that no precious space is wasted.

GROWING ON

Our propagator and greenhouse will be full all through the spring months, bursting at the seams with sprouting seedlings. A daily task is to reshuffle the trays, first from the warmth of the propagator to the bolstering action of the grow light. Once they have a pair or two of true leaves they can handle being pricked out into deep plug modular trays. They grow on, still in the shelter of the greenhouse, in bright light until there is no room or time for any more molly-coddling. By this time they have become stocky little plants and are hardy enough to spend a couple of weeks toughening up in the cold frame, after which, if the weather is favourable and the ground warm enough, they will be planted out.

PLANTING

To get perennial transplants off to a good start, we wait until the soil is flushing with annual weeds, a good indication that it is warm enough. We water them in well, until a small puddle forms around the plant, this helps to settle the soil particles in around the roots and keeps the plant in place. At this stage if you are still experiencing plummeting temperatures at night it really helps to cover the plants with a layer of fleece or mesh. Despite being hardy they do benefit from a bit of protection while rooting in.

STAKING

Thankfully the majority of perennials do not need staking, especially if they have been grown without the addition of lots of nitrogen-rich compost and have a good windbreak to protect them. For the ones that do need reinforcement,

the most efficient way is with a roll of plastic plant support netting at the same width as the bed. The key is to get this netting on while the plants are still young and small. One last weeding session before doing it is advisable and if irrigation is planned that should be in place. Stout wooden or metal stakes are banged in on the corners of our beds so that the netting can be pulled taut at around 45–60cm (18–24in) above the ground. For some particularly tall or floppy plants, a double layer is even better, which we provide for delphiniums and chrysanthemums. Another tip is to use tall bamboo canes along the row if it is particularly long to keep the netting taut and horizontal.

Above, left: Ash netting the delphiniums before they shoot skywards. He pulls the roll tightly over the posts to get as much tension as possible.

Above, centre: Threading two stock netting cages over a tripod of canes in readiness for an explosion of growth from *Clematis* × *durandii*.

Above: This giant of a perennial, *Persicaria alpina*, is sturdy enough to grow happily in an exposed part of our field without any support. It doubles up as a windbreak for the less wind-tolerant crocosmia and clematis on the other side.

SELF-SUPPORTING TALL PERENNIALS

Stem length is always welcome, but perhaps not the time-consuming task of staking plants that otherwise would be laid flat by high winds and rain. Perennials that are self-supporting save time and have the added advantage of saving on the plastic netting that we use on our cutting beds.

Ageratina altissima 'Braunlaub'
× *Alcalthaea suffrutescens* 'Parkallee'
Artemisia lactiflora 'Elfenbein'
Bidens aurea
Campanula lactiflora
Cephalaria gigantea
Echinops bannaticus
Foeniculum vulgare 'Purpureum'
Macleaya microcarpa 'Spetchley Ruby'

Persicaria alpina
Sanguisorba officinalis
Selinum wallichianum
Thalictrum 'Elin'
Veronicastrum virginicum

By mid-spring, new growth is gathering momentum in luminescent shades of green. I seek it out in framework branches of hazel, hornbeam and whitebeam, the radiant leaves just emerging, perfectly neat. Supporting blooms are supplied by flowering trees and shrubs, spiraea's twiggy sprays of froth, and a relay of blossom in the orchard, with blushed petals on the crabs and apples.

Perennials this early tend to be woodlanders, making the most of the light before the canopy greens over. Hellebores have ripened and muddied, encouraging the colour of spring-flowering bulbs to take centre stage, from the exotic crown fritillaries to their checkered and dusky understated cousins and the diversity and fragrance of the narcissi groups, swirls of creamy petalled doubles contrasting with the simplicity of the small cups. Spanish bluebells bring a cool, china blue into the selection – they are happy to be picked, unlike their English counterparts. The long wait is over; finally all the elements to create a mixed arrangement are ready and this verdant moment can be captured in the vase.

A handful of snakeshead fritillary, one of the most flattering spring accent flowers, it seems to elevate anything it is put with.

After a long winter my thirst for green is strong; hornbeam breaks into leaf before beech and the south-facing side of the hedge is first.

The wispy stems of bridal wreath are at their shapeliest before the tiny flowers fully open. I like to pick it when there is just a smattering of white.

BASAL CUTTINGS

These are essentially the same as stem cuttings except that they are taken from young growth at the base of the plant. Early spring is the best time for this, but it can be done at other times of the year by cutting the plant right back to create new growth artificially. If you plan to take a lot of cuttings from a favourite species it is useful to keep a stock plant in a large pot for this purpose. Take the cuttings as close to the crown of the parent plant as possible. We use modular trays, or crowd them together in a pot, which seems to promote a quick and vigorous root system. Bottom heat is beneficial, along with a moist atmosphere to reduce transpiration – for this I use very fine sheets of plastic, acquired from our local dry cleaners, and lay them over the trays of cuttings with wire hoops to keep them from resting on the leaves.

DIVISION

Dividing herbaceous plants is one of the oldest ways of making more and many of us are familiar with this method as a result of receiving a clump of plant

Right: The doughnut-shaped growth pattern of this *Cephalaria gigantea* is indicating that it's ready to be divided.

material from a fellow gardener. It is straightforward, with few risks, and an early spring division can yield more flowers or foliage in the same year. For cut-flower production, perennials need to be as vigorous as possible. Regular division, on average every three years, will encourage them to produce more stems and they will be better quality. We tend to focus on dividing plants that bloom after midsummer's day in the spring and plants that flower early in the year either in the summer or autumn.

THE CHELSEA CHOP

Named after the preparation of plants for the famous flower show, the Chelsea chop is a late-spring cut back by about a third. It is most effective on the more prolific, late-flowering perennials such as phlox, aster and sedum. In the border, this task is performed to keep perennials more compact and stop them flopping on to their neighbours; for the flower grower, it delays blooming so that a glut is avoided and makes the flowers smaller and more plentiful. Phlox panicles and sedum heads are also much easier to work with when their size is reduced.

Left: Cutting half our row of *Phlox* 'Mt Fuji' back by about a third avoids a glut and gives me spray-like stems of phlox with three smaller flowers on each stem later in the season.

The cusp between spring and summer is the greenest moment in the garden; new growth has been exponential and now, at its lushest point, waits to turn its energy to flowering. This green gap can be challenging for the flower grower and needs more planning than other times of the year. Flowering branches of lilac, viburnum and choisya are a lifeline for providing supporting flowers and, thanks to their shrubby size, they provide generous amounts. The first of the early-summer perennials such as geums, polemoniums and buttercups add scattered dots of colour, evoking a meadow feel which is easily enhanced with the black-leaved cow parsley and melica, one of the first grasses. Bold globes of allium add definition and bearded iris are welcome focal flowers in an array of plush velvety colours. All the fragrant flowers, of which there are many at this time of year, prompt nostalgia and are rather special for that reason. Lilac, honeysuckle, sweet rocket and lily of the valley are all reminiscent of past gardens and the people who tended and enjoyed them.

PICK OF THE GARDEN
Late spring

1 *Anthriscus sylvestris* 'Ravenswing' (black-leaved cow parsley)
2 *Allium hollandicum* 'Purple Sensation' (allium)
3 *Tellima grandiflora* (fringed cups)
4 *Convallaria majalis* (lily of the valley)
5 *Polygonatum* × *hybridum* (solomon's seal)
6 *Syringa vulgaris* (lilac)
7 *Hesperis matronalis* (sweet rocket)
8 *Iris* 'Pink Charm' (bearded iris)
9 *Lunaria rediviva* (perennial honesty)
10 *Choisya* × *dewitteana* WHITE DAZZLER (Mexican orange blossom)
11 *Viburnum opulus* 'Roseum' (snowball tree)
12 *Geum* 'Totally Tangerine' (geum)
13 *Polemonium* 'Lambrook Mauve' (jacob's ladder)
14 *Alchemilla mollis*
15 *Lonicera* × *americana* (American woodbine)
16 *Melica altissima* 'Alba' (Siberian melic)
17 *Ranunculus acris* 'Citrinus' (meadow buttercup)
18 *Viburnum opulus* (guelder rose)

Lily of the valley has such an evocative and powerful fragrance, just a few stems will fill a room with its scent.

The pale blue intermediate *Iris* 'June Prom' flowers before its taller cousins and its smaller flowers are easier to work into mixed arrangements.

Alliums are the last of the autumn-planted bulbs to flower. To suppress weeds, over plant with a slow-growing clump former such as *Geum* 'Totally Tangerine'.

Summer tasks

Summer is a relatively relaxed time of the year for the perennial cut-flower grower. If your cutting beds have been set up with an irrigation system and generously mulched then the two arduous jobs of watering and weeding will hopefully be a lot less work. This leaves time to focus on the most enjoyable and important task of these bountiful months: picking, conditioning and enjoying your flowers.

Above: Focal flowers together produce decadent, blousy displays reminiscent of a cottage garden. The depth of colour in *Clematis* 'Hudson River' cuts through the muted tones of *Rosa* 'Stephen Rulo'. It also acts as a framework element along with *Galega* 'Alba'.

Right: At the peak of summer, tall stems of *Echinacea pallida* with their drooping petals are backed by vertical slender spires of *Veronicastrum* 'Album'.

PICKING PERFECTION

There is an art to picking flowers so that you get the best from them and at the same time ensure any future flowers are not wasted. Over the years I have learnt that each plant has an optimum stage of harvest. The most common mistake is picking when the stem is too soft or unripe; it will wilt almost immediately and not recover. The flower is wasted, when a few more days might have been all that was needed for the stem to become more rigid and resilient. By grasping the stem just under the flowerhead and giving it a gentle wobble you can gauge how firm it feels. I have learnt that this takes a bit of practice, so as a general rule of thumb, make the cut when flowers are between one-third and halfway open. If the bees

Right: Delphiniums at the perfect stage for cutting with the bottom half of their florets open and tops still in bud.

Below: Giving an astrantia stem the wobble test. If it bends easily it probably needs another week.

have got there first and pollinated the flower it will fade quickly and is not really worth picking. Look for clean stamens without any signs of pollen. Petals tend to have a satin sheen when they are at their best, particularly noticeable in larger blooms such as roses, peonies and dahlias. It is a tactile task which I prefer to do without gloves, though they might be necessary for some plants with toxic sap.

The time of day is important. Harvest in the early morning or the evening, when the stems are most hydrated. I am an early riser, so I prefer the mornings when I have more energy and the plant cells are full of water after a period of darkness. Arm yourself with a clean plastic bucket of water and a pair of sharp snips – I always place my bucket in a shady spot close to where I am picking rather than leaving cut flowers sitting in full sun for any amount of time. Cut above a node or leaf joint to encourage the next crop of flowers. Next, strip the bottom half of leaves, since there will be more room in the bucket and with fewer leaves the stems are less likely to flop. Re-cut the stem at a sharp angle before placing it in the bucket. It is a good idea to choose the vase you are picking for first so that you can aim to cut at the right length and minimize waste.

Above: Peony 'Duchess de Nemours' waiting in the shade to be carried back to our cool shed. Their petals have a satiny sheen which tells me that despite being open they still give a few days vase life, so they are at the perfect stage for a wedding.

After a green pause in late spring, the abundance of flowers in early summer is breathtaking. This rush of colour feels quintessentially cottage garden – cool and soft tones of pink, blue and lilac. Form is dominated by spire shapes, giving both the border and vase a vertical thrust. Giants like persicaria and cephalaria are also reaching skywards and have already outgrown me. I enjoy feeling enveloped by the abundance and pick armloads of stems, attempting to capture the decadent mood of the garden in my arrangements. Of course it helps to have the real showstoppers of the perennial world at this time of year – the peonies, bearded iris and delphiniums all convene in early summer. I pull out my largest vases and use my arms at full stretch to accommodate this excess. There are plentiful supplies of textural supporting flowers from big producers such as lady's mantle (*Alchemilla mollis*), astrantia and the blushing lantern-like flowers of bladder campion (*Silene vulgaris*). To finish, a light touch of shimmering gold is provided from a few stems of giant oat grass (*Stipa gigantea*).

Cephalaria gigantea is at its best stage for picking when the pincushion centres are tight and green-tinged.

Clematis × *durandii* has the largest flowers of the herbaceous group. Its strong colour and form means it can hold its own as a focal flower in this arrangement with galega and foxgloves.

The variety of colour in peony cultivars is at its peak by early summer - from the deep red of *Paeonia* 'Buckeye Belle' to the hint of blush pink in the petals of *P.* 'Gardenia'.

CONDITIONING

This is the term used in the floral trade for preparing cut stems and allowing them to have a good rest and a long drink to prolong the vase life of the flowers. Once conditioned they will feel firmer, making them easier to arrange.

After picking, remove all the leaves that would be below the surface of the water and place the stems in a clean plastic bucket. This is to avoid bacterial build up which could clog their ends and prevent them taking up water. Now they are ready for a deep drink somewhere cool for at least three to four hours, ideally up to 12. We have a floral chiller but before that was installed our north-facing outside toilet was the best place.

Some flowers need special treatment to help them hydrate, which can be divided into the following categories.

A bucket of *Rosa* 'Port Sunlight' freshly picked and ready to go into the chiller for a long, cool drink.

SEARING FLOPPY STEMS

Some flowers and foliage struggle to take up water and will look rather sad and floppy after picking. Searing the ends is the best way to perk them back up and extend their vase life. Dipping the bottom few inches in boiling water breaks down the stems' outer layer, increasing the surface area able to conduct water. The most common time to do this is in the spring and early summer when new growth is soft and prone to wilting at the tips. The question of how many seconds to sear for can be answered by how soft the stems are, with woodies needing up to 30 seconds and softer material only 10. Have a bucket of deep, cool water ready to plunge the seared stems into up to their necks. This method can also be used on sap-producing stems such as euphorbias.

WOODY CUTS

To help woody branches take up water, make a vertical cross cut up the stem end using a pair of heavy-duty snips. This will split the stem open so there is more surface area available to take up water. Try to give woody cuts a longer drink, ideally 24 hours.

HOLLOW STEMS

Some flowers have drinking straw-like stems prone to air-locks which enter the stem when it is cut. To unblock, cut again under hot water and leave in the bucket to condition.

Clockwise from top left:
Sear stems in small bunches, these *Euphorbia amygdaloides* stems are held in a few centimetres of freshly boiled water for 20 seconds.

Making a vertical cross cut about 3cm (1in) long on a woody branch of magnolia opens up more surface area of the stem so that it can take up water quickly.

Some flowers and foliage benefit from full submersion, including hellebores, hydrangeas and smokebush, particularly if they are looking a bit floppy.

A hollow stem of *Persicaria alpina* (alpine knotweed) is recut under water to release any air bubbles.

SUBMERSION

Flowers and foliage with lots of surface area to their petals or leaves benefit from submersion. Float them in a large container of tepid water, push them below the surface and leave them for a few hours.

I do not use commercial flower food nor any of the kitchen-ingredient recipes to condition my flowers; I have always had great feedback on their freshness and longevity just from using plain water and the conditioning process. I think flower food is more relevant to imported stems which may have been harvested days ago when underripe. These often need extra help to look fresh and achieve full flower. If you're picking from your garden, all the stems will need is a resting period to drink, a clean vase, and a daily change of water.

It is the height of summer and the long, warm days have brought the perennials to their zenith. The field looks like an expanse of prairie-style planting, with paths engulfed by swathes of flowers, waist-high and swarming with pollinators. Horizontal plates of achillea contrast with spikes of caramel-coloured foxgloves and milky arching bellflowers. Bold daisy-shaped coneflowers, globes of agapanthus and echinops stand stiff and defined through a hazy screen of sea lavender and thalictrum.

The colour palette has expanded into warmer tones, with punchy corals, pinks and oranges provided by crocosmia, penstemon and phlox. So much choice means I want for little else but to combine all these contrasting forms in the vase, using the richer colours as eye-catchers. Roses take up the focal mantle, adding a feeling of decadence with their satin petals and delicious fragrance. Each cultivar has a unique scent and flower shape, making them feel very individual and a real treat to work with. They are so far removed from the sterile perfection of their hothouse cousins. Their relaxed, natural habit blends effortlessly with all the accompanying midsummer bounty.

The multitude of small thistles on each stem of *Eryngium* 'Blue Glitter' makes it an effective supporting flower.

My best performing rose 'Chandos Beauty' produces two generous apricot-pink flushes of flowers with a strong fruity scent.

Digitalis parviflora is a short-lived perennial but self seeds readily so there is always a good supply of these dense, rusty spikes to cut.

DEADHEADING

On a flower farm of this size it is impossible to pick every flower when it is ready, so weekly deadheading is inevitable. Fortunately most perennials and shrubs don't need this, which means less work and hopefully some seedheads and fruits to look forward to instead. The exceptions are roses and dahlias, which must have their spent blooms removed on a weekly basis so that energy can go into more flower production. In both cases it is beneficial to be bold and cut down into the plant to encourage long stem regrowth.

SUMMER DIVISION

Many early-flowering perennials can be divided straight after flowering; the plants are in active growth, so have plenty of time to bulk up their roots before

Below: Dead-headed dahlias give our compost heap a splash of colour at the start of each week. Regular dead-heading, along with feeding, ensures a consistent supply of quality cut flowers from our dahlias for a good three months. After just four days there will be plenty to pick again.

Right, clockwise from top left: An established clump of *Ranunculus acris* 'Citrinus' is split into twelve small divisions. Growing on these divisions in pots, in a sheltered position with regular watering, helps them to fill out a 9-cm (4-in) pot by early autumn, at which point they can be planted out and will flower the following year.

the winter. It is a bit of a radical approach but I find it speeds up the whole process – plants seem less likely to sulk and produce flowers more quickly the following year. As a flower farmer I want to get as much new stock out of a clump as possible, especially if it is the only plant I have. I use a pruning saw to make 'micro-divisions' and cut the foliage back. They are too small at this stage to fend for themselves, so I pot them up and grow them on in a cold frame or somewhere sheltered. By the autumn they will be ready to plant out.

CUT AND COME AGAIN

Perennials which flower in early summer can be encouraged to produce a second flush of flowers in the autumn, if they are cut back promptly. As soon as the crop is starting to fade, I shear it right down, leaves and all. It then needs a good watering and liquid feed to encourage fast, new growth and timely flowers.

SUMMER PRUNING

Shrubs that flower in late spring and early summer benefit from being pruned straight after flowering. This is because the new growth that follows will be next year's flowering wood and they need as long as possible to produce it. Most of the branches will have already been harvested, so it is a quick job to remove any old wood. This annual prune helps to maintain the plant's health and vigour, encouraging it to continue to be productive.

STEM CUTTINGS

I do not take many stem cuttings, just those of fast-growing shrubs and a few perennials which cannot be propagated in another way. In early summer, cuttings are soft or semi-ripe and should root rapidly. I select non-flowering, slender side shoots as I find these root more easily than chunkier ones. I always take as many as possible, aware that some will not root.

Below: To promote long, fine branches on *Spiraea arguta* I cut the older wood right back to the base of the plant.

Delphiniums in their second flowering flush in early autumn. They are half the size of their towering early summer spires which makes them easier to use in arrangements. The florets are also less densely packed giving the stems a lighter, more ethereal appearance.

By the end of summer, many plants have had their floral moment and are producing seedheads or waiting for a second flush of flowers later in the year. The garden can feel slightly weary and drab, but this is not really an option if you want a continual supply of flowers, particularly as it is peak wedding season. To avoid this lull, we focus on late-flowering perennials and grasses which will bridge the gap into autumn. Some are first-year flowering species, sown in early spring, which are characterized by height, texture and rich colour. Daisy-shapes reign in the form of rudbeckias, echinaceas and scabiosa. There is a lot of airy wafting movement from feathertop and smilo grass, hemp-leaved hollyhock and oenothera. The much-anticipated dahlias are finally getting into the swing of flowering, just in time, as the roses' first flush has run out of steam and a focal element is wanting. Shrubs are starting to produce fruit, the hypericum being one of the first, and I race to pick blackberry and raspberry branches before the birds get to them.

PICK OF THE GARDEN
Late summer

1 *Lathyrus latifolius* (broad-leaved everlasting pea)
2 *Origanum vulgare* subsp. *hirtum* (Greek oregano)
3 *Crocosmia* 'Lucifer' (montbretia)
4 *Helenium* 'Loysder Weick' (sneeze weed)
5 *Salvia* EMBER'S WISH (sage)
6 *Physostegia virginiana* (obedience plant)
7 *Oryzopsis miliacea* (smilo grass)
8 *Chelone obliqua* (twisted shellflower)
9 *Gypsophila paniculata* (baby's breath)
10 *Dahlia* 'Fairway Spur'
11 *Gaura lindheimeri* 'Whirling Butterflies'
12 *Hypericum × inodorum* MAGICAL UNIVERSE (St John's wort)
13 *Rudbeckia triloba* 'Prairie Glow' (brown-eyed susan)
14 *Echinacea purpurea* 'White Swan' (coneflower)
15 *Limonium platyphyllum* (sea lavender)
16 *Foeniculum vulgare* 'Purpureum' (bronze fennel)
17 *Pennisetum villosum* (feathertop)
18 *Scabiosa columbaria* subsp. *ochroleuca* (pale yellow scabious)
19 *Althaea cannabina* (hemp-leaved hollyhock)
20 *Rubus fructicosus* (thornless blackberry)
21 *Rudbeckia laciniata* (cutleaf coneflower)
22 *Hydrangea paniculata* 'Grandiflora' (hardy white-flowered hydrangea)
23 *Succisella inflexa* 'Frosted Pearls' (southern succisella)

The berries of *Viburnum opulus* are just starting to colour up, this wonderful two-tone effect is very versatile.

Echinacea 'Magnus Superior' flowers for two months, its intense magenta, horizontal petals followed by sombrero-shaped seedheads.

Dahlia 'Purple Flame' is a striking decorative type with its vivid magenta flowers and dark foliage that works well with supporting perennials.

Autumn tasks

Many flower farmers think of autumn as the beginning rather than the end of the flower-growing year. Work done now will reward the grower with plenty of flowers in the spring. It is a good time to make progress, when the soil is still warm, the light is mellow and tasks can be relished rather than rushed, as in the early part of the year. We get as much planted as possible – new perennials, shrubs and bulbs – while the ground is still warm. If your soil is well-drained and the winters are not too wet it is worth lifting and dividing early-flowering perennials. Perennials from seed can be sown now, especially those that need to experience winter temperatures for a prolonged period. They will sit in a cold frame and hopefully germinate in the spring. There is very little tidying or putting the perennial garden to bed for the winter, but I do like to take the tops off the roses, by about a third, to prevent wind rock.

Above: The second flush of roses combine well with dahlias. They are often slightly smaller and more intense in colour this time round so complement the dahlias beautifully. Here *Rosa* 'Port Sunlight' is combined with *Dahlia* 'Carolina Wagemans' and *D.* 'Peaches'.

Right: The low light of autumn adds a touch of gold to these seedheads of *Calamagrostis brachytricha*. Grasses literally shine at this time of year and are the main accent plant in arrangements.

Right: In autumn, narcissus bulbs are lifted from their shallow trenches in our holding bed and planted out in the field.

PLANT SPRING-FLOWERING BULBS

Each autumn we top up our spring-flowering bulbs, namely the narcissi and fritillaries. Most get tucked into yard troughs and planters where their cheery blooms will welcome customers to our farm gate in the spring. It is a good way to trial new varieties and once they have flowered they are dead-headed, transplanted into a holding bed and allowed to die back with their roots in

the ground before planting out in the field in autumn. For cutting, bulbs are planted very closely together, at 1–2cm (½–¾in) intervals. If you are planting in a bed, the easiest way to achieve such proximity is to dig a trench at about a spade's depth. Scatter some bonemeal in the bottom and then position the bulbs, water lightly to settle them in and backfill the soil.

Above: If the plan is to leave bulbs in situ then a trench should be dug to three times the depth of the bulb, which is about the depth of a spade. This planting depth also allows for overplanting with annual plug plants that flower later in the season.

As the days gradually shorten, so the range of plants for cutting begins to recede. Despite this slow fade there is still plenty of scale and texture available from the later-flowering perennials, woody cuts and grasses. The light is golden and the pace feels more relaxed. This is reflected in the harvesting which feels less restrictive, as we boldly cut longer stems. They have reached their ultimate height for the season and may not be needed again this year. It is time for the early-flowering perennials to put on a second flush, with delphiniums adding a striking note of blue to a colour palette dominated by warmer hues. The last of the perennials are mostly daisy-shaped. I try to select the smaller-flowered species with their starry sprays, such as *Rudbeckia triloba*. They soften the formality of the dahlias, which are producing an abundance of colour and bold form. The roses are back with their second flush, often richer in colour than the first, and the chrysanthemums are beginning to bloom – as we don't disbud them they are produced in smaller-flowered sprays. Woody cuts of ripened foliage and berries provide large, arching framework and supporting branches. They open up arrangements, accommodating a generous amount of these focal flowers and allowing me to make the most of this fleeting moment when they are all in bloom.

PICK OF THE GARDEN
Early autumn

1 *Solidago rugosa* 'Fireworks' (rough goldenrod)
2 *Rosa* HOT CHOCOLATE
3 *Persicaria alpina* (alpine knotweed)
4 *Astrantia major* (greater masterwort)
5 *Calamagrostis brachytricha* (Korean feather reed grass)
6 *Pennisetum orientale* 'Karley Rose' (oriental fountain grass)
7 *Jasminum officinale* (jasmine)
8 *Anemone × hybrida* 'Königin Charlotte' (Japanese anemone)
9 *Crocosmia × crocosmiiflora* 'Emily Mckenzie' (crocosmia)
10 *Chrysanthemum* 'Salmon Allouise'
11 *Clematis* 'Paul Farges' SUMMER SNOW
12 *Chasmanthium latifolium* (spangle grass)
13 *Bouteloua gracilis* 'Blonde Ambition' (Blue grama grass)
14 *Macleaya microcarpa* (plume poppy)
15 *Astrantia major* 'Ruby Wedding' (greater masterwort)
16 *Dahlia* 'Skyfall'
17 *Rubus idaeus* 'Autumn Treasure' (raspberry)
18 *Rosa glauca* (red-leaved rose)
19 *Hydrangea paniculata* 'Grandiflora' (hardy white-flowered hydrangea)
20 *Panicum virgatum* 'Rehbraun' (switch grass)
21 *Rudbeckia triloba* 'Prairie Glow' (brown-eyed susan)
22 *Ageratina altissima* 'Braunlaub' (snakeroot)
23 *Leycesteria formosa* (Himalayan honeysuckle)
24 *Bidens aurea* (Arizona beggar ticks)
25 *Sanguisorba* 'Cangshan Cranberry' (burnet)
26 *Delphinium elatum* 'Pink Blush'
27 *Symphoricarpos* Magical Charming Fantasy (snowberry pink)

The formal shape of ball dahlias is softened by pairing them with the looser decorative types and finished with seasonal branches of snowberry and grasses.

'Karley Rose' is a long-flowering pennisetum going from midsummer to early autumn if you pick it regularly.

Above, left: Harvesting the silvery seed-heads of *Catanache* 'Alba'. To ensure the seed is ripe, wait until the pointed tops have cracked open.

Above, centre: *Silene* seedheads are cut and placed in large paper sacks. They will be stored in the greenhouse to ripen off further and get rid of any excess moisture before they are cleaned.

Above, right: A horticultural sieve with a self-standing frame is used to separate the seeds from the chaff.

SEED SAVING

Seed is best collected on a dry, sunny afternoon when any morning dew will have evaporated. The seed of many mid- to late summer-flowering perennials will not be ripe until the autumn, so it is a race to harvest it before the wet weather sets in. The majority of plants produce generous amounts of seed, which means it is not necessary to remove every last seedhead. Some are as attractive as the flowers that preceded them, so I leave their sculptural shapes for cutting and as a food source for birds. I prefer to snip the seedheads into large paper sacks, which help to absorb any excess moisture. Most seed is collected when it has turned brown, which means it is ripe and ready to be shed, or in this case removed by hand. The next job is cleaning the seed for storage – it is important to do this promptly as seed capsules can retain moisture. This stage is called winnowing and can be done by gently blowing away the chaff or rubbing it through a sieve. As we collect seed to sell we are lucky to have mechanized this stage. It is then ready to store, for which I prefer to use small paper bags kept in airtight containers with a few sachets of silica. It is important to keep your seed stash somewhere that does not experience temperature fluctuations.

HARDWOOD CUTTINGS

This is the most relaxed way of propagating new plants as it is easy and has a good success rate, though cuttings do usually take a year to root. It is a good method for deciduous shrubs, species roses and fruit. Cuttings are best taken at leaf fall. Look for woody stems, not less than pencil-thick. Cut 20cm (8in) lengths with a sloping cut above a bud at the top and a cut straight across just below a bud at the bottom. Find a sheltered position to make a small trench, line it with grit and push them in. By the spring you should see new growth appear. It is important to not allow them to dry out, so water well during drier spells and and by the autumn they will have formed a strong root system and be ready to transplant.

Above, left: *Ribes* cuttings are pushed into a gritty trench in a nursery bed. This will be backfilled so only the top third of the cutting is above the surface.

Above, right: The following spring, the *Ribes* cuttings have begun to shoot. They will need to be kept weed-free and watered to survive the summer.

PUTTING THE DAHLIAS TO BED

Ideally, you should wait for a couple of killing frosts before cutting back all the top growth on dahlias. This helps the tubers to cure and toughen up for the winter. Check all the labels are still in place and legible. If there are any varieties you plan to propagate from in the spring, now is a good time to lift and store what I call the 'mother tubers' somewhere cool and frost-free. We shovel a generous molehill-sized pile of well-rotted compost on top of each plant, then an insulating layer of straw, at least 30cm (12in) deep. The tubers we store have the majority of the soil brushed off, after which they sit upside down to drain and dry off for a couple of weeks. This is important if they were wet when lifted. They are then stored in crates on a bed of potting compost with the tubers covered in chunky vermiculite. This naturally derived medium is very effective at maintaining humidity, so it helps to prevent tubers from drying out in storage.

Chrysanthemums can also be overwintered with a protective layer of mulch but we also lift a few plants, pot them up and overwinter them in an unheated greenhouse. In early spring a bit of heat will bring these stock plants into shoot. We take basal cuttings from the new growth, creating the next generation.

Opposite page: The dahlias have become sepia-tinted after a couple of hard frosts. We use a hedgecutter to make quick work of getting the bulk of the material off, it is then shredded onto the compost heap.

Left: The dahlias we have left in are all tucked up under a cosy blanket of compost and straw for the winter. This will be pulled back in mid spring when the shoots begin to appear.

The wild weather of autumn has arrived. It proves too much for the dahlias and roses, but some of the more sheltered chrysanthemums continue to carry the focal torch. The majority of perennials and grasses have finished flowering and are rushing to set seed in shapely ways. I pick them before they get too weathered and store them somewhere dry for use throughout the lean winter months. The rusty brown, tapered seedheads of willow-leaved loosestrife stand out against the straw-coloured plumes of Korean feather grass. I finally notice the perennial honesty, with its glowing horizontal slices of light. The echinacea has been picked clean of seed by the birds, revealing the bare bones of its cone centres. They look like miniaturized sombreros, such a transformation from a few weeks ago. Now is the time for deciduous shrubs and trees to take centre stage as they put on their autumn shades of gold, plum and copper. Some dazzle us with colourful foliage, while others produce shiny, bright fruits: the spindle, crab apple, hawthorn and the almost synthetic-looking beauty berry. Evergreens are looking fresh and bushy; after a summer of soft growth they are ripe and ready to be harvested. Eucalyptus, particularly *Eucalyptus nicholii* (willow peppermint) and herbs such as rosemary and scented geranium provide the fragrance.

PICK OF THE GARDEN
Mid and late autumn

1 *Rosmarinus officinalis* 'Miss Jessopp's Upright' (rosemary)
2 *Eucalyptus gunnii* (cider gum)
3 *Cortaderia selloana* (pampas grass)
4 *Cotinus* 'Grace' (smoke tree)
5 *Chrysanthemum* 'Spider Bronze'
6 Chrysanthemum 'Avignon Pink'
7 *Miscanthus sinensis* (silver grass)
8 *Chasmanthium latifolium* (northern sea oats), dried
9 *Spiraea thunbergii* (Thunberg spiraea)
10 *Chrysanthemum* 'Bigoudi Purple'
11 *Abelia* × *grandiflora* (glossy abelia)
12 *Fagus sylvatica* (beech)
13 *Jasminum officinale* (jasmine)
14 *Symphoricarpos* MAGICAL GALAXY (snowberry)
15 *Pelargonium* 'Lady Plymouth' (scented geranium)
16 *Alstroemeria* 'Inca Ice' (Peruvian lily)
17 *Euonymus europaeus* (spindle)
18 *Spiraea nipponica* 'Snowmound' (snowmound)
19 *Lysimachia ephemerum* (willow-leaved loosestrife) seedhead
20 *Physocarpus opulifolius* 'Dart's Gold' (ninebark)
21 *Chrysanthemum* 'Tula Sharletta'
22 *Eucalyptus nicholii* (willow peppermint)
23 *Weigela* 'Florida Variegata' (weigela)
24 *Hedera helix* (ivy)
25 *Brachyglottis* (Dunedin Group) 'Sunshine' (senecio)
26 *Sambucus nigra* (elder)
27 *Callicarpa bodinieri* (beauty berry)
28 *Leycesteria formosa* (Himalayan honeysuckle)

Chrysanthemums are making a come back. This is 'Tula Improved', its flash of red at the centre of each petal picks up the autumnal colouring on foliage perfectly.

Lysimachia ephemerum is one of my favourite seedheads. I cut the coppery tall tapers for both autumn and, because it stands so well, winter arrangements.

The dangling clusters of coral berries on *Berberis* 'Georgei' weigh down the branches into pleasing arching forms. They don't seem particularly interesting to birds so stay on the branches for a long time.

Winter tasks

Unlike many people, I look forward to winter, for the garden's dormancy allows for some much-needed rest and quiet reflection. The beauty of hardy perennials and shrubs is that they can be left all winter to fend for themselves. A good cold spell is welcomed by growers, who know it will mean fewer pests and more flowers. Indeed some plants, including peonies and roses, require a period of chilling to be at their most productive. Nothing gets tidied in the autumn – all of the stems and seedheads are left intact. They act as a wintery framework to display crystalline hoar frosts and offer valuable refuge to wildlife. However, by late winter the desire to clear up all the detritus from last year is overwhelming. It is time to revitalize the garden and our muscles for the full-on rush of spring ahead.

Above: A hoar frost highlights the wispy, twisting shapes of *Spiraea arguta* branches.

Right: The field in midwinter at its most dormant with the previous year's growth left as a protective cover. It is a useful time of year to note the gaps and make plans for spring planting.

The miscanthus is one of the last plants we cut back and for this job the hedgecutter works well on its dense clumps. We leave some of the material to protect the new shoots from spring frosts, which Jesse appreciates.

CUTTING BACK AND MULCHING

The first job of the year is cutting back all the winter-worn top growth to make way for the fresh new shoots to come. It gets piled up for a few days to give any winter residents time to move on. Throwing all this woody material on to the compost heap would be too much, turning it dry and dormant, so we use a shredder to break it down into small pieces which helps to activate the rotting process.

After cutting back comes mulching. To save time and money, weeding and watering are two jobs we try to keep to a bare minimum, and the most effective way of achieving this is to cover the beds with an organic material that will suppress weeds and lock in the moisture. It protects the soil from the elements while feeding and improving its texture. On a more superficial level it makes the cutting beds look shipshape and ready for the season ahead.

Mulch can be whatever is to hand, as long as it is weed-free and not too high in fertility, as you will be applying a generous layer annually. For perennials, grasses and bulbs we use municipal green waste, which is everyone's garden clippings composted to a high temperature. It is completely sterile, light to handle and most importantly easy for us to get delivered directly into our field.

For our trees and shrubs we plant into a narrow strip 50cm (20in) wide which is mulched with ramial wood chips, made from young woody growth. We chip our own from the material accumulated from pruning and cutting back the shrubs

Left: *Rosa glauca* has been mulched with freshly chipped wood from branches brought down on the farm by a storm.

Below: Winding back to the previous winter when the *Rosa glauca* went in the ground as a bare root plant sourced cheaply through a hedging company. It is getting a dusting of mycorrhizal fungi powder before it goes into a generous sized hole which allows its roots to spread out.

and hedges on the farm. It decomposes more quickly than larger wood chip, enriching the soil at the same time while effectively suppressing the weeds for an entire year.

BARE-ROOT PLANTING

If there is the option to buy plants bare root I will always take it, as they are cheaper and have a larger root system than their containerized counterparts. Trees, particularly fruit, hedging, roses and some perennials including peonies, bearded iris and phlox can all be sourced as open-ground stock. It is a good way to buy plants online and certainly saves on postage for nurseries offering mail order.

Bare-root plants need time to settle their roots before the light and warmth trigger their top growth, so it is preferable to get these planted in early winter – of course the weather usually dictates when there is a mild window of opportunity. We have a nursery bed where bare-root plants are heeled in and wait it out. Before planting, give the roots a good soak, for at least an hour for woody cuts. As you plant, dust the roots with mycorrhizal fungi powder. This will help the plants to develop a root system that is highly efficient at absorbing water and nutrients from the soil. It is important not to use bonemeal if you are applying mycorrhizae as its high phosphorus content will stop the fungi from flourishing and doing its good work.

Above: This spiraea had become very dense and overcrowded with short twiggy branches. I was no longer picking it and it was crowding out the neighbouring plants. I removed almost half of its growth down to ground level, thinning out the older branches and opening up the centre of the plant. It will not be very productive this year but I should have plenty to pick off it after that.

PRUNING

The dormant season is a good time to carry out a number of different pruning techniques in order to manage the size of trees and shrubs and keep them in productive condition.

Formative

Firstly there is formative pruning on young woody plants. By taking out the leading stem, known as the apical bud, growth is redirected to numerous side branches lower down. This helps to keep trees and large shrubs within easy reach. With all the energy going into the laterals instead of skyward, they will grow to a usable length.

Renewal

Removing old, unproductive branches, often down to the ground, will encourage new growth. If you prefer a kinky shape to your stems I recommend doing this every two to three years, so you can enjoy a combination of older more characterful branches for vase arrangements and the new straighter growth for bouquet work.

Rejuvenation

If a shrub has been neglected and appears to have run out of steam it might need rejuvenating by cutting all the stems down to ground level. It is similar to coppicing but is not done on a regular basis. The plant will respond by producing vigorous, long, straight stems which will be ready to harvest the following year.

Late-flowering shrubs

Woody plants such as roses, hydrangea and snowberry are pruned in late winter. This gives them time to produce new wood, which is what they will flower or fruit on from midsummer to the autumn. If they are pruned hard they will produce fewer stems but larger flowers. I find these supersized blooms look out of place in a naturalistic arrangement, so I prune further up the plant to encourage smaller flowers and more of them.

Coppicing

This is the practice of pruning almost completely down to the ground. Although plants that are coppiced grow back quickly, it is pretty severe treatment and a couple of years will pass before they are in full production again – a good reason

Above: I used to prune this row of *Hydrangea paniculata* 'Limelight' almost down to the ground but the super-sized blooms that resulted from this approach were too unwieldy. I now take just half the plant back to a bud and a permanent framework has developed over the years which is a useful reminder of where to make the cut.

Opposite page: *Eucalyptus parvula* during the process of pollarding. These trees will now need a good water and feed to encourage plenty of new growth. The deadline for making the cut is the spring equinox so it is a good idea to harvest plenty through the winter months.

Right: *Salix gracilistyla* one year on from coppicing has produced very straight, whippy stems a good 1.5m (5ft) tall.

to have more than one plant and adopt a rotational system. The advantage of this treatment is that it encourages faster growth and prolongs the life of the plant. For plants grown for their foliage it can rejuvenate the colour of the leaves and increase their size. The new growth generated by coppicing will be very straight with little branching. In general, fast-growing deciduous species of trees and shrubs are good candidates for this technique. How frequently and how low to cut does vary, but as a general rule cut back every three years to about 15cm (6in) above the ground. A plant should be at least a year old before it is coppiced so that it has developed a healthy root system. After pruning, give it a good feed with a mulch of organic matter.

Pollarding

This is carried out for the same reasons as coppicing and is a similar technique but done higher up the plant. It is useful when you want to raise the new shoots, perhaps if you have a problem with rabbits or need space for shade-loving plants, which could be tucked underneath. Select the main trunk of the plant, removing any other leaders or suckers at the base. I tend to cut at waist height which is approximately 1m (3 ¼ft) high. It is important that the trunk is at least 5cm (2 in) in diameter and no bigger than 13cm (5in) when you pollard for the first time.

Once I have caught my breath after a busy season, winter normally begins with foraging evergreens and bare branches for Christmas wreaths. I always include eucalyptus and larch, the latter's whippy branches studded with small nut brown cones adding direction and movement. It is then time for a break until the end of winter when the garden is showing signs of emerging out of its dormancy, the birdsong has started again and I can feel a whisper of spring in the air. There are welcome patches of brightness in the general drab: the golden tassels of hazel and rosy catkins on the japanese pink pussy willow, and snowdrops scattered in groups in our woodland area spearing the sodden earth, to flare out their milky blooms. Scent catches you unawares at this time of year, from the discreet flowers of sweet box and winter honeysuckle – just a couple of branches are enough to perfume a room. If I am feeling really self-indulgent I will pick a few hellebores, knowing that this early they are too soft and will only last a day or two. The appreciation for every flower, leaf and twig is much deeper at this slower time of year. I am inclined to arrange each genus singly or in a simple pairing, as it suits how they look in the garden, standing out in solitary beauty.

As another growing season draws to an end it feels good to know that all the tasks are completed and represent an investment into an ongoing supply of flowers and foliage for years to come.

Snowdrops poke up through the arum leaves, they make good border and vase companions. The arum leaves are small enough to use at this stage and have attractive marbled leaves.

Using a base of grapevines woven into a hoop, I make a simple christmas wreath of *Eucalyptus gunnii*, cone-studded larch twigs and dried limonium. I finished it with a silk ribbon dyed with walnut bark.

The first pussy willow catkins to pick are pink ones from *Salix* 'Mount Aso'. Enjoy these ones fresh as the colour slowly fades to grey as they dry.

Plant directory

This selection of 128 plants covers the majority of perennials and woody plants I have tried and tested on our flower farm. It is by no means a comprehensive list on the subject and is biased towards plants that are trusty performers with a relaxed attitude and natural style.

The directory is divided into five plant groups: **bulbs**, **perennials**, **climbers**, **grasses** and **trees and shrubs**. Within these categories the plants are in alphabetical sequence. Each category is described from my perspective as a grower of cut flowers and I have tried to capture how each one contributes to the plant palette.

Each entry begins with the botanical name, which I have used because common names often differ regionally. This is followed by the common name I am familiar with. A brief description of the plant's essential characteristics and preferred growing conditions follows. It includes my observations on why it has made the cut, which can range from its colour, form or high yield to its contribution of something special and timely to an arrangement. Many plants come with a backstory, sometimes including from whom or where I bought it, which will hopefully be a useful sourcing reference.

HEIGHT: This is given with regular harvesting and pruning for cut flower use in mind. The height will always be shorter than its garden equivalent, particularly in the case of woody cuts which need to be kept within arm's reach.

RECOMMENDED PLANTS: These are species or cultivars within the same genus as the plant listed, selected to extend the selection that you grow. If you have grown to particularly like a plant or find that it thrives on your site, you will probably want to extend your range.

SPACING: This indicates the planting distance, again with regular harvesting in mind, which will be much closer than in a garden setting.

CULTIVATION TIPS: Here I focus on advice specific to cut flower cultivation and offer tips and tricks you can use to make a plant more productive, timely and the right shape and size for your floristry. For general plant care, see Seasonal Tasks pages 80-131.

WHEN TO HARVEST: I recommend the best time to harvest for optimum vase life and indicate here if there is more than one season to harvest, for example spring growth, summer flowers, autumn berries or foliage.

CONDITIONING AND VASE LIFE: Conditioning techniques are provided in brief here, refer to page 100 for full information. In general, I consider vase life to be good if the plant lasts at least five days.

USES: These are the key contributions the plant makes to an arrangement, which can include the time of year, its colour, form, design element and what it pairs well with.

PROPAGATION: Propagation techniques are provided in brief here. Refer to pages 82-3 and 90-91 for further information. If a plant is slow-growing or difficult to propagate I advise on sourcing instead.

Bulbs

The plants listed over the next few pages all grow from bulbs which readily naturalize, blooming year after year. Bulbs make it possible to extend the flowering season, particularly at the beginning of it when these precious spring jewels give the most joy after the emptiness of winter.

Autumn-planted bulbs are the lifeblood of our farm, providing the majority of our flowers until the annuals and perennials come into bloom in late spring. Some, including tulips and ranunculus, are treated as annuals. As much as I love them, it is a costly process to replace them every year, both financially and environmentally. By expanding my bulb repertoire into perennial bulbs it means I need to grow fewer of the higher-impact annuals.

With the exception of some of the double narcissus, most of the spring-flowering bulbs listed are not as flamboy-ant as the ones we treat as annuals. They tend to be smaller, more subtle, performing as supporting or accent flowers. As they are some of the earliest pickings in the garden, I often arrange them on their own, where their detail and delicacy can be fully appreciated. In comparison, summer-flowering bulbs are bold in colour and form. I could have included agapanthus and crocosmia in the perennial section of this plant directory, but I often source them as bulbs, which is a lot cheaper when you need larger quantities for cutting.

Once planted, perennial bulbs demand very little attention apart from occasionally lifting and dividing clumps to maintain a good flower size and productive crop. The main issue with growing bulbs perennially is managing the weeds which will happily take advantage of the bare ground the bulbs leave behind after flowering.

Overplanting with low, spreading perennials is a good way to make the most of the space and deter weeds. Alliums are very happy with an understorey of geum, stachys or alchemilla. As narcissi leaves die back, they leave room for later-flowering half-hardy annuals such as cosmos and nicotiana, which can be tucked in as plug plants in early summer. Another way to keep the bed clean is to cover it with landscape fabric once the foliage has died back; the bulbs can stay dormant like this until the autumn. The cover should then be removed so the bulbs have time to vernalize through the colder winter months.

To ensure a good harvest of flowers the following year, leave the foliage and pick only the flowering stems. Most flowers produced from bulbs have a long vase life – if picked in bud they will happily grow on and become more characterful in the vase for a good two weeks.

Agapanthus
African lily

I grow African lilies for the timely nature of their flowers, particularly the blues, which in mid and late summer are a highly prized colour. The flowers are rounded umbels composed of numerous little trumpet-shaped florets and are mainly in the blue and violet-purple spectrum, with a few whites. There are some good hardy varieties that will clump up in three years given space and a sunny position that is moist but well-drained.

RECOMMENDED PLANTS: These are all strong-growing, free-flowering forms.
A. 'Ardernei Hybrid' – large white with blush-pink tips to petals and black anthers. H 80cm (2½ft)
A. 'Cheney's Lane' – pale blue. H 1.2m (4ft)

A. Headbourne hybrids – the hardiest form. H 70–90cm (2¼–3ft)

SPACING: 30cm (1ft) apart.

WHEN TO HARVEST: When just a few florets are open.

CONDITIONING AND VASE LIFE: Remove dead florets as they age; 14 days

USES: The taller forms with their sturdy stems and bold flowers make good focals in a stately arrangement and pair well with spire shapes. Smaller forms are good mixers with dahlias, opening up the dahlias' solidity with their airy globes.

PROPAGATION: I am always looking for quantity so tend to buy mine as rhizomes from a bulb supplier, I pot them up and grow them on before planting out. If you are looking for something particular, choose them when they are in flower. Divide established clumps in the spring.

Agapanthus 'Ardernei Hybrid'

Allium hollandicum 'Purple Sensation'
Allium

I do not grow many alliums as I find their spherical flowerheads and lollipop-like stiff stems do not really suit my loose, fluid style. However, I am prepared to overlook this for their timely flowering, which fills the gap between spring and summer. The allium season can be extended into late summer with the smaller-flowered forms, which are also easier to work into arrangements.

RECOMMENDED PLANTS:
A. stipitatum 'Mount Everest' – a statuesque white variety, with tennis ball-sized flowerheads adored by bees. H 1.2m (4ft)
A. 'Summer Beauty' – small, cool mauve, pompom flowers in late summer, long-lasting and loved by bees. H 60cm (2ft)

SPACING: 15cm (6in) apart

WHEN TO HARVEST: Pick before the flowers have fully rounded out.

CONDITIONING AND VASE LIFE: To minimize the smell of onions, you can add a drop of bleach to the water. 14 days.

USES: A focal for late spring with foxgloves, bearded iris and black-leaved cow parsley.

Left: *Allium hollandicum* 'Purple Sensation' interplanted with *Geum* 'Totally Tangerine'.

Below: *Allium stipitatum* 'Mount Everest' showing the beginnings of its beaded, green seedheads.

PROPAGATION: Alliums self-seed and naturalize. We started with about a hundred *A.* 'Purple Sensation' bulbs 12 years ago and now have about 5 times that number. The richly coloured violet umbels will revert to the paler mauve species when they naturalize.

Convallaria majalis
Lily of the valley

This low-growing woodlander has a fleeting flowering period and vase life, but its fragrance and elegance are so exquisite that it should definitely be considered if you have a shady spot with moist soil. The rhizomes are slow to establish, but if they are happy and you are lucky they can naturalize. Plant in early autumn in clumps of 10–15 crowns in a partially shady border. H 23cm (9in)

RECOMMENDED PLANTS:
C. majalis 'Fortin's Giant' has larger flowers and the advantage of flowering two weeks later than the species to extend the season. H 30cm (1ft)

SPACING: 15cm (6in) apart.

ANNUAL CARE: Mulch in the autumn when the leaves die back.

WHEN TO HARVEST: The bell-shaped flowers should be open apart from a few at the top and look pure white. Cut the flowers and leaves together.

CONDITIONING AND VASE LIFE: 5 days.

USES: Enjoy their delicacy as a single-type arrangement, their strong green leaves acting as a natural complement to the bright white flowers. I find a vintage crystal bud vase befits their old-fashioned charm.

PROPAGATION: By division in early spring every 3-4 years.

Convallaria majalis, simply arranged with its leaves which act as a foil for the flowers.

Crocosmia
Crocosmia

These bulbous perennials are a favourite for mid- to late summer cutting, their brilliant, hot colours tempered by the delicacy of the arching spikes of starry or funnel-shaped flowers. They enjoy moist soil and dislike drying out.

RECOMMENDED PLANTS: One could easily develop a crocosmia habit – I have seven and counting, with the aim of prolonging their flowering season from midsummer to early autumn.
C. 'Lucifer' – the earliest, tallest and most vibrant vermilion red. H 1.2m (4ft)
C. × crocosmiiflora 'George Davison' – mid-season, rich amber yellow, freesia-like flowers. H 90cm (3ft)
C. × crocosmiiflora 'Emily McKenzie' – late-flowering, star-shaped, orange flowers with a deep red blotch at the base. H 60cm (2ft)

SPACING: 25cm (10in) apart.

CULTIVATION TIPS: To keep costs down, buy them as corms, potting them up in the spring and letting them fill the pots with roots before planting out. Plant deeply to help them overwinter in cold areas and stop them drying out during the summer.

WHEN TO HARVEST: Cut stems when the first two or three florets are open. They can also be used for their sculptural seedheads.

CONDITIONING AND VASE LIFE: If the water is kept fresh some of the buds will continue to open indoors. 7 days.

USES: Their strong feathered form and colour make them an elegant focal in meadow-style arrangements and they can also play a supporting role with dahlias.

PROPAGATION: Divide every 4 years in spring.

Fritillaria uva-vulpis
Fox's grape fritillary

A bulbous perennial with clusters of dusky purple bell-shaped flowers adorned with golden tips. One of the easiest and most cost-effective fritillaries to grow, it likes a sunny, well-drained spot. I grow it in pots with plenty of additional grit. H 30cm (1ft)

RECOMMENDED PLANTS:
The chequered *F. meleagris* can also be forced in pots; plant it deeply and keep it shady and moist when dormant. It is an accent plant which adds a sour note to the sweetness of spring.

SPACING: Plant closely, almost touching.

WHEN TO HARVEST: As buds are just opening.

CONDITIONING AND VASE LIFE: 7–14 days.

USES: A spring accent to add movement and sultry style to tulips and ranunculus. The colouring pairs beautifully with hellebores and amelanchier.

PROPAGATION: Lift bulbs after foliage has died back and divide.

Fritillaria uva-vulpis, the dusky purple to mahogany flowers have an unusual frosted blueish sheen akin to bloom on grapes, hence its common name.

C. × crocosmiiflora 'Emily McKenzie' with its elegantly arching starry flowers are a pleasing shade of burnt orange, an apt colour for this late-flowering variety.

Crocosmia × crocosmiiflora 'George Davison'

Crocosmia × crocosmiiflora 'Emily McKenzie'

Galanthus
Snowdrop

Snowdrops make surprisingly good cut flowers, especially if they have large petals and long stems. What better way to appreciate these diminutive beauties than in the comfort of a warm home in late winter? They seem to enjoy being indoors, flaring their outer petals to reveal pencilled green underskirts while exuding a delicious honey scent.

RECOMMENDED PLANTS:
G. 'Atkinsii' – a showy variety with large, pendulous flowers and long stems. Strong-growing, bulks up readily. H 25cm (10in)
G. 'S. Arnott' I was fortunate to be given a clump of this exceptionally large, single-flowered cultivar many years ago. It is vigorous, clumping up quickly, so

Galanthus 'Atkinsii'

now it is dotted through our orchard border, where it enjoys the partial shade and heavy soil. H 25cm (10in)

SPACING: 5cm (2in) apart.

WHEN TO HARVEST: Just before the buds open.

CONDITIONING AND VASE LIFE: 7 days in a cool room.

USES: These exquisite flowers excel in fresh little clusters arranged on their own in simple bud vases.

PROPAGATION: Lift and divide clumps 'in the green' after they have flowered but before the foliage has started to die back, this is usually in early spring. Replant smaller clumps at the same depth.

Hermodactylus tuberosus
Widow iris, snake's head iris

A subtle yet alluring flower with many common names that attempt to describe its grassy green standards and black velvet falls. I planted this tuberous perennial in a south-facing raised bed 15 years ago; it has slowly naturalized into a large grassy clump enjoying the sun-baked position and well-drained soil. H 20cm (8in)

SPACING: 10cm (4in) apart.

WHEN TO HARVEST: Pick stems while in bud in early spring.

CONDITIONING AND VASE LIFE: 10 days.

USES: Enjoy the detail, delicacy and scent of this stylish flower on its own in a small bowl of water with a pin holder at the bottom to anchor the stems.

PROPAGATION: Divide as soon as the leaves die back in early summer.

Hermodactylus tuberosus

Hyacinthoides hispanica
Spanish bluebell

A reliable and robust version of its wild cousin, known as scilla in the cut-flower trade. The round stalks are studded on all sides by broad, bell-shaped flowers. For good stem length and flower colour, grow in dappled shade. H 45cm (17½in)

RECOMMENDED PLANTS:
H. hispanica 'Excelsior' – pale blue.

SPACING: 10cm (4in) apart.

WHEN TO HARVEST: For the longest vase life, pick just before the bells start to open.

CONDITIONING AND VASE LIFE: I tend to pluck mine and then cut above the white part of the stalk, which does not take water up well. 14 days.

USES: One of the first blue flowers and spike forms of the season, this supporting flower is a valuable mood- and shape-changer in mid to late spring arrangements.

PROPAGATION: Divide established clumps in late summer.

Left: The stems are harvested when the majority of bells are still closed.

Below: *Hyacinthoides hispanica*

Narcissus
Narcissus

Signalling the beginning of the flowering season, this surprisingly diverse genus is one of the most perennial of bulbs. I have some that have been growing happily in the same spot for more than ten years. Narcissi are hardy, easy to grow and rarely plagued by pests and diseases. If you select varieties from across the different categories (known as Divisions) you will have flowers to pick from early to late spring. Many are fragrant, and sunny yellow is certainly not the only colour available; there are narcissi with petals in snow white, ivory and primrose yellow and trumpets and cups in peachy-pinks, apricots and tangerine orange. The forms are equally varied, ranging from the many-layered petals of doubles to the understated stylish Poeticus and small

cups through to the split coronas and multi-headed blooms of Jonquillas and Tazettas. When planting the doubles, try to find somewhere relatively sheltered. Some varieties do very well in grass, which solves the dilemma of what to do with a bed once they have finished flowering. Alternatively, overplant with biennials a month after the bulbs have gone in.

Opposite page, top: *Narcissus poeticus* var. *recurvus* is the last variety to flower in late spring, perfect timing for this elegant combination with Solomon's seal.

Opposite page, below: *Narcissus* 'Segovia' in a yard trough.

Below: Picking from our field rows of narcissus sheltered by the cutting hedge.

RECOMMENDED PLANTS:

N. 'Actaea' – a well-known Poeticus variety; I love the natural species look of this group. One of the best for scent and vase life. Late season. H 45cm (17½in)

N. 'Geranium' – a prolific and reliable Tazetta variety, with very fragrant, creamy petals and tangerine orange cups. Mid season. H 40cm (15½in)

N. 'Pink Charm' – a large cupped daffodil with ivory outer petals and coral- rimmed trumpets. Mid season. H 40cm (15½in)

N. 'Replete' – a popular double with ivory petals inlaid with coral ruffles. Early season. H 40cm (15½in)

N. 'Segovia' – small and delicate open-faced flowers with pure white petals and a soft lemon, crimped flat cup. Late season. H 20cm (8in)

SPACING: 10cm (4in) apart.

CULTIVATION TIPS: Deadhead any unpicked flowers to prevent energy going into producing seed, this will help to bulk up the bulbs.

WHEN TO HARVEST: When the flowers are in bud, have filled out and bent over into the nodding 'goose neck' stage. Avoid cutting leaves as the bulb will need these to produce flowers the following year. I tend to pluck my stems rather than cut them – it gains stem length and less slimy sap is exuded.

CONDITIONING AND VASE LIFE: Their sap is toxic to other flowers and will make a mixed arrangement go over more quickly. To avoid this, condition them separately and then do not recut the stems when you arrange them. 10 to 14 days.

USES: I think the easiest way to get round the rather unfriendly nature of narcissus is to arrange them on their own. If you have many varieties it is fun to showcase them in clusters of small vases.

PROPAGATION: Lift and divide the bulbs after four years to increase the stock, renew their vigour and improve flower size. The best time to do this is after flowering when they are 'in the green' and will root in more quickly.

Every year we trial new varieties of narcissus in our tunnels and yard troughs. If I decide they are keepers they are transplanted into our field rows.

Left: 'Peach Swirl', one of the best doubles, offering large flowers with white petals and an egg-yolk yellow centre. It has strong stems and a long vase life.

Opposite page, top row left to right: 'Tommy White', 'Bridal Crown', 'Frosty Snow', 'Segovia', 'Peach Swirl', 'Actaea'.

Middle row left to right: 'Art Design', 'Thalia', Split-corona type peach, 'Pink Charm', 'Geranium'.

Bottom row left to right: 'Geranium', 'Cool Flame', 'Actaea', 'Frosty Snow', Split-corona type peach, Split-corona type yellow.

Perennials

Perennials are the gardener's cut flower, bringing a more naturalistic feel to arrangements. A true floral expression of your garden through the seasons, they can liberate your arrangements from looking similar to others or, dare I say it, like shop-bought flowers. The majority of perennials listed here are hardy herbaceous types. Essentially this means they are plants with non-woody stems that live for more than two years. A herbaceous perennial produces new growth every year, flowers, and then dies back to the ground over winter, becoming dormant until the following spring. They are all frost-hardy here on the farm in Oxfordshire, which is in an area that often records the lowest temperatures in England.

I have included dahlias and chrysanthemums, which are classed as tender perennials, but with the milder winters we are experiencing I have found they can be left in the ground, with the protection of a deep mulch. This approach not only saves on time and storage space but will reward you with earlier flowers.

Many of these perennials are well known garden plants, readily available and adaptable to a wide range of growing conditions. Reliability, weather tolerance and vigour are important plant attributes for the flower farmer – plants need to thrive to produce enough to harvest.

The peak flowering period for perennials is midsummer to early autumn, but there are outliers which help to extend the season, with asters in mid-autumn and some hellebores coming into flower in late winter. In contrast to the fleeting nature of annuals, many perennials can reward for years. Some, such as peonies, last for decades, with very little intervention, though most will need to be propagated, in the simplest form by division, to keep them in a healthy, productive condition. The most prolific are often short-lived, first-year-flowering species such as achillea, which are easily raised from seed, but start to fade away

Digitalis parviflora

after three years. On the farm, we grow more species of perennials for cutting than any other plant group. There is an almost limitless range to experiment with and I can always find the perfect fit for a gap in my palette. Most can be defined as supporting flowers – they have an understated, relaxed character and often bear a close resemblance to their wild cousins. I use them to naturalize my

arrangements and soften the more eye-catching focal flowers. Over the next few pages, you will find 65 of my favourite perennials. They are all tried-and-tested, performing well in the garden and the vase. It is not a definitive list, just a starting point to inspire you to build your own personal perennial collection.

Achillea
Yarrow

One of my staple first-year-flowering perennials to grow from seed, *Achillea* is short-lived in our rich soil and wet winters, becoming washed out and unproductive by the third year. To overcome this I sow it annually and have two highly productive crops on the go, a first and a second year, which gives me a good succession of harvestable stems from early to late summer. It likes full sun and well-drained soil.

RECOMMENDED PLANTS:
A. millefolium 'Colorado' – a mix of warm shades, so a good variety for lots of colour choice in a small space. H 60cm (2ft)
A. millefolium 'Summer Pastels' – an array of pastel shades, lots of peach, buff and cream so a good one if you are growing them for a wedding. H 60cm (2ft)
A. ptarmica (The Pearl Group) 'The Pearl' – elegant sprays of pure white, pom-pom flowers. H 60cm (2ft)
A. sibirica subsp. *camschatica* 'Love Parade' – lilac-pink flowers with yellow stamens. H 45cm (17½in)

SPACING: 30cm (1ft) apart.

CULTIVATION TIPS: Clear after 2-3 years and replace with new plants to maximize production.

WHEN TO HARVEST: When florets are fully open and have good colour and the stem feels ripe.

CONDITIONING AND VASE LIFE: 10 days.

USES: This is one of our staple supporting flowers. I love the faded Persian carpet colours of the species *A. millefolium*, which have a shade that works for every arrangement. The plate-like flowers are a good horizontal form to contrast with the many vertical spires around at this time of year; I prefer to use the smaller heads, which are easier to incorporate. They are excellent for drying.

PROPAGATION: By seed in early spring. When in flower, label your favourites, then lift and divide plants in the spring to make larger blocks of single colours.

Achillea millefolium 'Summer Pastels'

Ageratina altissima 'Braunlaub'
Snakeroot

This plant produces umbel-like clusters of small off-white flowers from late summer to early autumn. The flowers are displayed on mahogany stems with leaves like nettles in a pleasing mid-green. Grow in part-shade and moist soil.

RECOMMENDED PLANTS:
A. altissima 'Chocolate' – dark, pewter-purple foliage with buff flowers. H 1.2m (4ft)

SPACING: 45cm (17½in) apart

WHEN TO HARVEST: Before the flowers have fluffed out, which quickly leads to discolouration. They should be in tight, creamy-green buds.

CONDITIONING AND VASE LIFE: 7 days.

USES: A staple supporting flower that is an excellent substitute for an umbel-shape. The foliage is also a handsome addition to bouquets.

PROPAGATION: By basal cuttings or division in early spring.

The refreshing creamy green flowers of *Ageratina altissima* 'Braunlaub' balance the richer colour palette of late summer.

× *Alcalthaea suffrutescens* 'Parkallee'

One of my best purchases from the famed Orchard Dene Nursery in Oxfordshire, this tall, herbaceous mallow/hollyhock cross is a robust plant with a long flowering period in late summer that far surpasses hollyhock season. It will continue to produce shorter side stems when the primary stem is cut and is more rust-resistant than its biennial cousins. The flowers are apricot-pink fading to cream, with ruffled centres and burgundy anthers. Each one is positioned with plenty of space along the stems, giving them a light, airy appearance. H 1.5–2.4m (5–8ft)

RECOMMENDED PLANTS:
× *A. suffrutescens* 'Parkfrieden' – apricot pink, double centred flowers. H 1.5m (5ft)

SPACING: 45cm (17½in) apart.

WHEN TO HARVEST: When half the florets on the stem are open.

CONDITIONING AND VASE LIFE: 7 days.

USES: It is surprisingly versatile, for besides the tall, spire-shaped stems for large arrangements, the shorter side branches are a stylish, neutral supporting flower from midsummer to early autumn.

PROPAGATION: By softwood cuttings in early summer. I take a few every year as they tend to be short-lived, especially in a wet winter.

× *Alcalthaea suffrutescens* 'Parkallee'

Alchemilla mollis
Lady's mantle

A popular plant among flower arrangers for good reason: it is a staple supporting flower in early summer, producing an abundance of stems without any fuss. I prefer to grow my plants in part shade to prolong the chartreuse-green colouring, which I think is more flattering to other flowers than a sun-bleached yellow-green. H 40cm (15½in)

SPACING: 30cm (1ft) apart.

CULTIVATION TIPS: Cut back straight after flowering to encourage a smaller second flush in the autumn and to prevent self-seeding.

WHEN TO HARVEST: Once half the flowers on a stem are open. If you prefer to use it for its scalloped leaves, the stems can also be picked in bud.

CONDITIONING AND VASE LIFE: If in bud, sear for 10 seconds. 10 days.

USES: A frothy supporting flower for country-style arrangements.

PROPAGATION: To ensure the plants remain productive divide in the autumn every 3 years.

The honey-scented froth of *Alchemilla mollis* is enjoyed by pollinators.

Alstroemeria
Peruvian lily

Flowering for months in the garden and weeks in the vase, this workhorse of the cut-flower world has had its reputation sadly tarnished by its association with supermarket flowers. Thoughtful variety selection can circumvent the shop-bought look. I tend to gravitate towards the smaller-flowered varieties with simple colouring. Plant in full sun in fertile, well-drained soil.

RECOMMENDED PLANTS:
A. 'Apollo' – striking contrast of white edged green outer petals and yellow-flushed inner petals with mahogany flecks. H 80cm (2½ft)

A. 'Elvira' – buff-pink with brown flecks. H 90cm (3ft)
A. 'Friendship' – soft yellow flushed with pink. H 90cm (3ft)
A. psittacina – the parrot lily, with narrow trumpet flowers in crimson-tipped bright green. H 1m (3¼ft)

SPACING: 45cm (17½in) apart.

WHEN TO HARVEST: Early summer and again in early autumn. Harvest the stems by pulling them, like rhubarb. This encourages further flowering. I prefer the shape and colour of the flowers when they are just beginning to open.

CONDITIONING AND VASE LIFE: Strip the stems of foliage, wearing gloves as the sap can irritate the skin. 14–21 days.

USES: The loose clusters of flowers are just the right shape to nestle around larger single focal flowers. Their prolonged flowering period from early summer to the first frosts allows for plenty of different partnerships.

PROPAGATION: It is better to start again with new plants than to attempt division as they resent disturbance.

Alstroemeria 'Apollo'

Amsonia
Blue star

An easy and adaptable plant which I mainly grow for the golden willow-like foliage in the autumn, *Amsonia* produces starbursts of milky blue flowers in early summer that are very welcome too. They tend to be slow-growing plants and will take a couple of years to reach their full clump size. Position in full sun.

RECOMMENDED PLANTS:
A. 'Blue Ice' – dense panicles of pale blue flowers from slate buds, yellow ochre leaves in autumn. H 50cm (19½in)
A. hubrichtii – billowing mounds of fine, thread-like leaves, the best for autumn colour. H 70cm (2¼ft)

The pale blue flowers of *Amsonia* 'Blue Ice' make a striking contrast with the darker buds.

A. tabernaemontana var. *salicifolia* – dense clusters of ice-blue flowers on arching stems. H 90cm (3ft)

SPACING: 30cm (1ft) apart.

WHEN TO HARVEST: When half the flowers in the cluster are open or when it is in full autumn colour; it holds onto its leaves well after cutting.

CONDITIONING AND VASE LIFE: Sear to contain the milky sap. 10 days.

USES: An elegant and refreshingly different supporting flower or foliage.

PROPAGATION: By side shoots after flowering.

Anemone × *hybrida*
Japanese anemone

Japanese anemones are an indispensable late-autumn-flowering perennial for bringing the freshness and purity of spring to the mellowness of autumn. They will take a couple of years to get settled in before they produce a good harvest, which is more likely in dappled shade and moist but well-drained soil. I prefer the semi-double forms, which seem to have a longer vase life.

RECOMMENDED PLANTS:
A. × *hybrida* 'Königin Charlotte' – large, semi-double soft pink flowers.
H 80cm (2½ft)
A. × *hybrida* 'Robustissima' – a vigorous plant with light pink flowers.
H 80cm (2½ft)
A. × *hybrida* 'Whirlwind' – small, semi-double white flowers.
H 80cm (2½ft)

SPACING: 30cm (1ft) apart.

WHEN TO HARVEST: Once the flowers are fully open, but before the pollen starts to shed.

CONDITIONING AND VASE LIFE: Sear for 20 seconds; 7–10 days.

USES: I enjoy the opportunity for contrast that these anemones bring to arrangements. The pastel shades of their flowers are like a breath of fresh air amid all the rich opulence of dahlias and berried branches.

PROPAGATION: By division in spring or root cuttings in autumn if eelworm is an issue.

Anemone × *hybrida* 'Königin Charlotte' produces tall branched stems of large semi-double flowers over a period of two months.

Anthriscus sylvestris
'Raven's Wing'
Black-leaved cow parsley

The gothic version of cow parsley, with its deep plum stems and leaves which create a dramatic contrast to the creamy-white lacy umbels. A stylish addition to the late spring border and the vase. H: 90cm (3ft)

RECOMMENDED PLANTS: *Anthriscus sylvestris* – cow parsley

SPACING: 30cm (1ft) apart.

WHEN TO HARVEST: Stems should feel firm, with open umbels.

CONDITIONING AND VASE LIFE: Sear for 20 seconds and condition overnight. 7 days.

Anthriscus sylvestris 'Raven's Wing'

USES: The fern-like leaves make a wonderful filigree collar for early spring arrangements. For the flowers, make the most of their tall, airy nature and pair them with other long-stemmed flowers in season such as bearded iris and sweet rocket.

PROPAGATION: I allow mine to self seed: in early spring I select the darkest seedlings as soon as they produce their first true leaves, prick them out and grow on in pots. It is a good idea to do this every year to ensure plenty of flowers as they are short-lived perennials.

Anemone × *hybrida* 'Robustissima'

Anemone × *hybrida* 'Whirlwind'

Aquilegia chrysantha
'Yellow Queen'
Columbine 'Yellow Queen'

I wish I could grow lots of columbines as they make such wonderful late spring cut flowers but sadly our site is infected with the dreaded aquilegia downy mildew. Interestingly, this species does not seem so affected by it and happily it is also one of the most vigorous and long-lived. It is also exceptionally beautiful – large, upward-facing, bright lemon flowers are furnished with dramatic sweeping spurs. It does best in light shade and moist but well-drained soil. H 60cm (2ft)

RECOMMENDED PLANTS:
A. 'Kristall' – a pure white flower, with long spurs. H 60cm (2ft)

SPACING: 30cm (1ft) apart.

WHEN TO HARVEST: As flowers are opening, before they are pollinated.

CONDITIONING AND VASE LIFE: Sear; 5 days.

USES: The colour and form are bold enough to warrant a focal position in arrangements. Pick out the shades of yellow by pairing them with giant scabious and meadow buttercup. For a dramatic contrast I grow and arrange them with black-leaved cow parsley.

PROPAGATION: By seed, ideally fresh, in early summer. If you are saving seed, be aware that columbines hybridize very readily if there are other species or cultivars close by. Plant out in the autumn.

The spurs of *Aquilegia chrysantha* 'Yellow Queen' add movement and direction.

Artemisia lactiflora 'Elfenbein'
White mugwort

I was introduced to this plant on a visit to Orchard Dene Nurseries – the owners knew my business well and always made astute suggestions of what might work for cutting. This German selection has a fresher, more elegant appearance than the species. 'Elfenbein' translates as 'ivory' which describes the generous, creamy sprays of flowers which arch over at the top of upright stems. It is very welcome in late summer when there is a plethora of weddings to supply. H 1.2m (4ft)

RECOMMENDED PLANT:
A. lactiflora Guizhou Group has purple-flushed foliage and stems. H 1.2m (4ft)

SPACING: 45cm (17½in) apart.

WHEN TO HARVEST: Cut when there are clean tight buds, before the flowers begin to look dirty.

CONDITIONING AND VASE LIFE: 7 days.

USES: A feathery supporting stem with dahlias and late summer daisy-shaped perennials.

PROPAGATION: By division in early spring.

The creamy-white sprays of *Artemisia lactiflora* 'Elfenbein' add a fresh note to late summer displays.

Aruncus dioicus
Goat's beard

An accommodating, handsome plant which is rather like a giant wispy astilbe. I find it much easier to grow in our dry conditions and prefer its wilder form. In early summer it produces large, creamy, feathery spires above light green pinnate leaves. It can be grown in full sun if the soil is moist.

RECOMMENDED PLANTS:
A. 'Horatio' – large sprays on self-supporting stems, good autumn colour. H 1m (3¼ft)

SPACING: 45cm (17½in) apart.

WHEN TO HARVEST: Before it becomes too frothy – the flowers should look tight and beaded. The graceful seedheads and

coral-tinted foliage make it a worthwhile cut stem in the autumn too.

CONDITIONING AND VASE LIFE: 7 days.

USES: The graceful, tapering plumes add a lightness of touch to all the blousy, fullness of early summer, linking the garden to a more relaxed, meadow feel.

PROPAGATION: By seed or division in spring or autumn.

The tall plumes of *Aruncus dioicus* 'Horatio' are the perfect supporting flower for delphiniums.

Astrantia major
Great masterwort

Astrantia's star-shaped ruffs crowned with pin-cushion centres remind me of vintage costume jewellery. The multi-flowered stems are the archetypal supporting flower, adorning arrangements with their intricate beauty. It is a stalwart of the cutting garden, but only if you can provide it with moist, heavy soil and preferably partial shade. These conditions will yield a bountiful harvest in two productive, long-stemmed flushes in early summer and late autumn.

RECOMMENDED PLANTS:
A. m. 'Large White' – our strongest grower, with large rayed greenish-pink flowers. H 75cm (2½ft)
A. 'Roma' – a Piet Oudolf selection, rose-pink flowers with good repeat flowering. H 60cm (2ft)
A. m. 'Ruby Wedding' – deep ruby-red flowers. H 60cm (2ft)

Astrantia major

SPACING: 30cm (1ft) apart.

CULTIVATION TIPS: Cut back straight after flowering, water and feed to encourage a second flush of flowers in early autumn.

WHEN TO HARVEST: The central flower must be fully open and the stem should feel firm and ripe. If there is a musty smell they have been pollinated and are going over.

CONDITIONING AND VASE LIFE: 10 days.

USES: They are the perfect accompaniment to blousy peonies, roses and dahlias, adding a detailed delicacy to an arrangement.

PROPAGATION: By seed or division in spring or autumn.

Bidens aurea
Arizona beggar tick

This was given to me by a fellow flower grower – it spreads quickly, so it is easy to pass it on. It has become one of my favourite supporting flowers for late summer to early autumn. Loose sprays of creamy, primrose-yellow flowers are borne on tall, willowy stems from fern-leaved clumps. The flowers look similar to small cosmos and have an appealing vanilla fragrance. They are easy to grow and hold up well without staking. This plant is happiest in full sun and well-drained soil. H 1.5m (5ft)

RECOMMENDED PLANTS:
B. aurea 'Hannay's Lemon Drop' – shimmering bright, lemon-yellow flowers with white-tipped petals. H 1.5m (5ft)

SPACING: 45cm (17½in) apart.

WHEN TO HARVEST: Once half the flowers are open on the stem.

CONDITIONING AND VASE LIFE: 7 days.

Bidens aurea has branching stems covered in masses of delicate daisy-like flowers.

USES: Make the most of their height and graceful habit and arrange them in prairie style with grasses, umbels and other daisy-shaped flowers in different sizes, such as aster and coneflowers.

PROPAGATION: By division in spring.

Campanula
Bellflower

One of my favourite genera for good cut-flower candidates, this summer-flowering cottage garden classic comes in seasonally appropriate shades of blue, lilac, pink and white. They tend to be quite diverse in their form and stature but all have a bell-shaped flower in common, whether it is hanging in elegant silhouette or upright in full, blowsy clusters. They are hardy and easily pleased, growing happily in fertile, well-drained soil in full sun or part-shade.

RECOMMENDED PLANTS:
C. IRIDESCENT BELLS ('Iribella') – shining purple buds open into large, luminescent, silvery-lilac bells. It has *C. takesimana* in its breeding but boasts more stem length and a longer flowering season. H 75cm (2½ft)
C. lactiflora – the milky bellflower forms large clumps of tall stems laden with clustered bell-shaped flowers. There are a number of good cultivars to choose from, including 'Loddon Anna', with large flowerheads of smokey lilac-pink and the stylish 'Platinum', a silvery grey with pewter sepals. It is one of the most reliable, long-lived and productive perennials that I grow, needing plenty of space. H 1.5m (5ft)
C. 'Sarastro' – inky-blue elongated bells hang from slender stems, flowering from mid to late summer. H 60cm (2ft)
C. takesimana – arching sprays of tubular hanging bells, lilac-white flushed plum. Easy from seed, flowering in its second year. H 50cm (19½in)

SPACING: 30cm (1ft) apart except *C. lactiflora* at 45cm (17½in).

WHEN TO HARVEST: Once half the flowers are open.

CONDITIONING AND VASE LIFE: 10–14 days.

USES: Arching stems with hanging bells excel in pared-back displays where their serene outline can be appreciated. They work beautifully with foxgloves and umbellifers. Clouds of milky bellflower are one of the best supporting and complementary flowers for roses.

PROPAGATION: By division in spring or autumn.

Above: *Campanula takesimana* 'Alba' are cream with maroon spotting inside the bells.

Right: *Campanula lactiflora* 'Loddon Anna' produces large full flowerheads on sturdy stems.

Catanache caerulea
Cupid's dart

A first-year-flowering perennial that produces a sea of violet-blue papery, fringed, cornflower-like blooms, from early to late summer. This European native is loved by pollinators and makes a valuable addition to relaxed meadow-style arrangements. If it is planted in a sunny position in well-drained soil I have found it can be very productive for a good three years. H 60–90cm (2–3ft)

RECOMMENDED PLANTS:
C. caerulea 'Alba' – creamy white with a deep violet centre. H 60–90cm (2–3ft)

Below: *Catanache caerulea*

Left: *Catanache caerulea* 'Alba'

SPACING: 30cm (1ft) apart.

WHEN TO HARVEST: The flowers close at night so wait until they are fully open before picking.

CONDITIONING AND VASE LIFE: 7 days.

USES: The dark centre of the flowers creates a punchy accent. I particularly like the stylish *C. caerulea* 'Alba', which I find more versatile. The silvery-scaled seedheads on their slender stems are a useful textural element and dry beautifully.

PROPAGATION: By seed in early spring or autumn.

Cephalaria gigantea
Giant scabious

A 'love at first sight' plant – it was early summer and the uniquely coloured scabious-like flowers were alive with bumble bees. I knew it would always have to be included in any garden I created and it has turned out to be very good for cutting. The lime-green buds open to pale yellow- green flowers that are produced on tall, branching, self-supporting stems. An easy and fast-growing clump former, it prefers full sun and moisture-retentive soil to produce plenty of harvestable stems. H 2m (6½ft)

Below and right: *Cephalaria gigantea*

RECOMMENDED PLANTS:
C. dipsacoides – paler cream flowers in midsummer. Self-seeds freely. H 1.5m (5ft)

SPACING: 50cm (19½in) apart.

WHEN TO HARVEST: The pincushion centres should be tight, in other words before the flowers are pollinated.

CONDITIONING AND VASE LIFE: Hollow stem. 5 days.

USES: Mimic its lofty stature in the vase, letting it hover above the other flowers as an airy accent.

PROPAGATION: By division in spring.

Chrysanthemum
Chrysanthemum

I am so pleased that chrysanthemums are experiencing a renaissance; they certainly deserve more recognition for their ability to provide flowers from early to late autumn, in a sumptuous array of painterly colours and forms. I was persuaded to reconsider them after a trip to Japan, where they are deeply revered. No self-respecting park or garden was without elaborate displays of varieties that were unlike anything I had ever seen.

Chrysanthemums can be tender or hardy – I mostly grow decorative and spider forms which are tender. Probably because of our milder winters, some of these cultivars cope well with being left in and mulched, in a similar way to dahlias. They do need to be grown in well-drained soil and a sunny, sheltered position for this approach to be successful. As a contingency I always lift and containerize a few plants, as stock, and overwinter them in a frost-free greenhouse. If you don't want the fuss, or you grow on heavy clay, then it is worth exploring the Rubellum and Korean types which are completely hardy, even flowering after a light frost. These tend to produce informal sprays of smaller daisy-shaped or pompom flowers.

RECOMMENDED PLANTS:
C. 'Avignon Pink' – best described as a nude pink, decorative form, controversially a late-season indoor variety, but by overwintering it outside it will flower earlier. H 1.2m (4ft)
C. 'Pandion Bronze' – a coppery decorative form, with a long flowering period. H 1.2m (4ft)
C. 'Percy Salter' – sprays of sea anemone-like flowers of a light biscuit colour. Very weatherproof. H 90cm (3ft)
C. 'Salmon Allouise' – an early intermediate, with incurved petals in a soft salmon, highly productive. H 1.2m (4ft)
C. 'Spider Bronze' – the name describes it perfectly. H 1.2m (4ft)
C. 'Mary Stoker' – a Rubellum type, with single apricot-yellow daisies with fine rays, flowering early to late autumn. H 90cm (3ft)

SPACING: 45cm (17½in) apart.

CULTIVATION TIPS: Cut back in early summer to about 20cm (8in) to encourage strong, bushy growth and more stems with smaller flowers. Feed regularly. Support the plants by growing them through netting, preferably in two layers.

WHEN TO HARVEST Once half to two-thirds of the flowers are open.

CONDITIONING AND VASE LIFE: Conditioning and vase life: An impressively long vase life of up to 21 days.

USES: The single-headed blooms with their incurved or spidery petals make magnificent autumnal focal flowers. Combine them with dahlias and late-flowering roses, then add a backdrop of eucalyptus with fluffy grasses, berries and clematis seedheads for texture and accent.

PROPAGATION: By division or basal cuttings in early spring.

CHRYSANTHEMUM KEY

1 'Tula Improved'
2 'Salmon Allouise'
3 TULA SHARLETTA
4 BIGOUDI BRONZE
5 'Allouise Pink'
6 GILBERT LEIGHT SILVER
7 'Spider Bronze'
8 BIGOUDI PURPLE
9 TULA CARMELLA
10 TARANTULA RED
11 BIGOUDI RED
12 'Avignon Pink'
13 'Pandion Bronze'
14 'Daily Mirror'
15 'Hanneburg'

Far left: *C.* 'Pandion Bronze'

Left: *C.* 'Salmon Allouise'

Clematis
Herbaceous clematis

I overlooked herbaceous clematis for many years, presuming they would be like their climbing cousins – almost impossible to pick and with a short vase life. After discovering imported stems of BLUE PIROUETTE at the flower market I realized that they did in fact last for a good two weeks in the vase. Further breeding has produced a good range of both star- and bell-shaped varieties in shades of white, blues, pinks and purples flowering in early summer. Herbaceous clematis are non-climbing so will need a practical support system which keeps their floppy stems upright but allows for easy picking. We use cylindrical cages made of galvanized stock netting. They like warm shoots and cool roots, so partial shade and deep, fertile soil are ideal.

RECOMMENDED PLANTS:

C. 'Arabella' – a profusion of small star-shaped, mauve-blue flowers, a long flowering period. H 2m (6½ft)

C. BLUE PIROUETTE – another gem from the Amazing series, with deep violet-purple, medium-sized, upward-facing, twisting sepals. H 1.5m (5ft)

C. × durandii – my most productive clematis, bearing large, star-shaped flowers in a rich indigo blue with contrasting creamy-yellow anthers. H 1.8m (6ft)

C. EAST RIVER – known as 'Amazing London' in the cut-flower world, with star-shaped flowers in pale lavender with creamy anthers. H 1.5m (5ft)

C. 'Rooguchi' – very smart, long, ribbed bells in a rich shiny purple with silvery-purple margins. H 2m (6½ft)

C. TWINKLE – dainty white bell-shaped flowers with pale blue crowns and gently twisting sepals. H 1m (3¼ft)

SPACING: 1m (3¼ft) apart.

WHEN TO HARVEST: As the sepals begin to open. Some varieties are followed by attractive fluffy seedheads in the autumn.

CONDITIONING AND VASE LIFE: Cut the stems long enough to retain some of the woody section – this will help the stems to take up water. After conditioning overnight they can be cut to the desired length. 14 days.

USES: I normally manage to take 30–45cm (12–17½in) in stem length when harvesting clematis. The star-shaped varieties make stunning focal flowers alongside garden roses, while the refined nature of the bell-shaped varieties works more effectively as supporting flowers.

PROPAGATION: Buy 2-year-old plants from a specialist clematis nursery.

Below: A row of *Clematis × durandii* is the largest flowering herbaceous clematis so works well as a focal flower.

Right, clockwise from top left: *Clematis* 'Rooguchi', *Clematis* 'Hudson River', *Clematis* 'East River', *Clematis* 'Arabella'.

Dahlia
Dahlia

Dahlias are essentially tender perennials but I leave the tubers in over winter here, where they have coped surprisingly well with occasional flooding and freezing temperatures. They are a key focal flower for us, providing our shop and event work with an abundance of stems to pick for a good three months from late summer to first frosts. Not only are they hard-working and generous but, with recent breeding, the range of colours and forms available is breathtaking.

One of the reasons I leave the tubers in the ground over winter is to close the focal flower gap that can occur in midsummer, when the roses finish their first flush. Dahlias that have been growing away in the ground since the spring will

flower a good month earlier than their lifted counterparts. The quality of the flowers will diminish after three years, as the tubers become overcrowded; the flowers will revert back to singles and become thin in the neck, washed-out in colour and prone to viruses. It is at this point that I clear the bed and start again, always on new ground, in full sun and fertile soil.

RECOMMENDED PLANTS: It is easy to develop an out-of-control dahlia habit, so a few guidelines are helpful on

Left: *Dahlia* 'Preference' a small, semi-cactus type in a soft peachy-pink.

Below: *Dahlia* 'Wine Eyed Jill'

selecting the right varieties for cutting. I always look at the stem length first; ideally, it should be over 90cm (3ft) to ensure good, clear stems. Look for varieties recommended for their vigour and productivity. Most of my dahlias fall in the small to medium-size range with a few dinner-plates and at the other end of the scale some miniature pompoms. For shape I like a core of looser forms such as the decoratives, water-lily and anemone-flowered dahlias. I add in a smattering of fluffy cactus types and finally, for something more punchy, accents of small ball, pompom and single or collarette forms. My most useful varieties are the ones that are versatile and blend well with other colours:

D. 'Café au Lait' – the queen of dahlias needs no introduction; a large decorative creamy coffee sometimes with blush tints, the perfect neutral. H 1.2m (4ft)

D. 'Carolina Wagemans' – my longstanding favourite, a perfect waterlily form with flowers which open apricot turning to a glowing pinky-peach. Masses of long stems. H 1.2m (4ft)

D. 'Dark Spirit'– a lustrous maroon pompom. I prefer flowers in this rich, velvety colour to be smaller and less intrusive. H 80cm (2½ft)

D. 'Josudi Andromeda' – all of the Josudi series are cactus forms which are good for cutting, 'Andromeda' is a miniature cactus, blush lilac, tall. H 1.4m (4½ft)

D. 'Nulands Josephine' – large pompom, rhubarb and custard colours, long stems. H 1.2m (4ft)

D. 'Penhill Dark Monarch' – a large decorative with ruffled petals in smoky-plum. H 1.5m (5ft)

D. 'Salmon Runner' – a two-toned raspberry and coral decorative with a lighter edge to the petals. H 1m (3¼ft)

D. 'Seniors Hope' – dusky rose with raspberry-wine backs to the petals. This dahlia seems to improve any arrangement I add it to. H 80cm (2½ft)

D. 'Westerton Pearl' – small ball in a soft, antique pink. H 1.2m (4ft)

D. 'Wine Eyed Jill' – small decorative, soft, creamy peach with deep wine centres. H 1.2m (4ft)

SPACING: 50cm (19½in) apart each way in a double staggered row.

CULTIVATION TIPS: Cut back after a couple of heavy frosts and mulch with a molehill-sized mound of compost and a thick duvet of straw. In mid-spring, pull the straw back and apply some slug control. If a frost is forecast just push the straw back over to protect the tender shoots.

WHEN TO HARVEST: Flowers must be fully open as they will not continue to unfurl in the vase. Check the backs of the flowerheads, which should look and feel

Left to right: *Dahlia* 'Purple Flame' with vivid purple-red flowers and contrasting bronze foliage; *Dahlia* 'Sandia Shomei', a delicate, lavender waterlily with long stems; *Dahlia* 'Carolina Wagemans' blends apricot and peachy-pink in its full waterlily-shaped flowers.

satiny. Be bold and cut down into the plants so that stems are at least 30cm (1ft) long. This encourages strong regrowth from the base, rewarding you with more long stems the following week. On the farm we harvest our dahlias twice a week as this keeps them growing strongly and cuts back on deadheading.

CONDITIONING AND VASE LIFE: Recut under hand-hot water and leave in to condition. The pompom and ball-types have the longest vase life, of 5–7 days.

USES: Dahlias feature heavily in all of my arrangements from midsummer to the first frosts, which means they enjoy a whole host of supporting flowers and foliage which are selected to pick out their colours and to soften and 'naturalize' their bold, rather formal shapes. I normally use a selection of three to five varieties that contrast in form and size but are harmonious in colour.

PROPAGATION: By dividing the tubers or taking basal cuttings from lifted ones in early spring.

Top row left to right: 'Witteman's Best', 'Jowey Winnie', 'Porcelain', 'Babylon Brons', 'Kiwi Gloria', 'Sweet Nathalie', 'Little Robert', 'Preference', 'Henriette', 'Islander', 'Wine Eyed Jill', Tartan, 'Josudi Andromeda'

Middle row left to right: 'Darkarin', 'Silver Years', 'Lavender Perfection', 'Seniors Hope', 'Mambo', 'Brown Sugar', 'Kelsey Annie Joy', 'Nulands Josephine', 'April Heather', 'Mister Frans', 'Genova', 'Zundert Mystery Fox' 'Merlot Magic', 'Café au Lait'

Bottom row left to right: 'Christopher Taylor', 'Evanah', 'Take Off', 'American Dawn', 'Diva US', 'New Baby', 'Hillcrest Royal', 'Rancho', 'Cornel Brons', 'Polka NL', 'Penhill Dark Monarch', 'Sandia Shomei', 'Purple Flame', 'Josudi Hercules', 'Salmon Runner', 'Peaches', 'Linda's Baby', 'Ivanetti', 'Arbatax', 'Zippity Do Da', 'Carolina Wagemans', 'Preference'

Delphinium elatum
New Millennium Series
Delphinium

The majestic spires of these New Zealand hybrids have far out-performed any other delphinium I have tried to grow. I originally grew mine from seed posted from the other side of the world by the breeder Terry Dowdeswell a decade ago and they are still going strong. Their tall stems carry a dense covering of large florets in a range of soft and deep shades from dusky pinks and green-tinged whites to deepest indigo purples and turquoise blues. Their growth is vigorous and sturdy. They are very hardy and cope well with high temperatures in the summer. The first flush produces some towering spires which are a little daunting, but the second crop is half the size and easier to work with. Position in a sheltered, sunny position in rich soil. H 1.5m (5ft)

RECOMMENDED PLANTS:
D. 'Black-eyed Angels' – semi-double white with a striking black bee.
D. Dusky Maidens Group – semi-double dusky pink with brown bee.
D. elatum 'Morning Lights' – semi-double soft lilac with white bee.
D. 'Pagan Purples' – semi-double rich purple with brown bee.

Below left: Second flowering with smaller spires in early autumn.
Below: *Delphinium* 'Pagan Purples'
Bottom: *Delphinium* 'Black-Eyed Angels'

For a smaller, more delicate alternative: *D.* (Belladonna Group) 'Völkerfrieden' – branching flowering stems have a loose, informal habit with widely spaced florets for a more elegant effect. 'Cliveden Beauty' is a clear sky blue and 'Casa Blanca' a creamy white. H 80cm (2½ft)

SPACING: 50cm (19⅓in) apart.

The New Millennium Series in full colour range behind and the more delicate Belladonna Group in front.

CULTIVATION TIPS: Cut back in the autumn and mulch generously. Once growing, they will need sturdy support to stop heavy winds and rain felling them, ideally with two layers of netting. Cut back as soon as the first flush starts to fade, then water and feed to encourage a second flowering in early autumn.

WHEN TO HARVEST: Once the lower half of the florets are open.

CONDITIONING AND VASE LIFE: Re-cut the hollow stems under warm water. They are ethylene-sensitive, so try to keep them away from other flowers and fruit. 7 days.

USES: Perfect for large-scale, stately arrangements used generously with a contrasting light supporting flower.

PROPAGATION: By seed or basal cuttings in early spring.

Digitalis
Foxglove

Most of the foxgloves I grow for cutting are cultivars of the well-known biennial *D. purpurea*. There are many other species that are short-lived perennials, all of which are spire-shaped but differ quite widely in colour, stature and habitat. Some are sun-lovers that come into flower a bit later, their slender spires in golden honey and coppery browns, reflecting the warmth of high summer. Wear gloves when handling any of this genus as all parts of the plant are toxic and can enter the body through absorption.

RECOMMENDED PLANTS:
D. grandiflora – buttery-yellow trumpets with bronze freckled throats, light shade. H 75cm (2½ft)
D. obscura 'Sunset' – short wiry stems of rusty-brown bells with orange throats, full sun. H 45cm (17½in)
D. lanata – tawny brown with large white lip, full sun or part-shade. H 60cm (2ft)
D. parviflora – caramel-coloured densely packed short trumpets on slender, tapered spires, full sun. H 90cm (3ft)
D. × mertonensis – large bells the colour of crushed strawberries, part shade, divide after flowering to keep it perennial. H 90cm (3ft)

SPACING: 30cm (1ft) apart.

WHEN TO HARVEST: Early to mid summer. All foxgloves are loved by bees but when they are pollinated the flowers drop quickly, so pick when just a few bells are open. Cut the primary flower to encourage shorter secondary stems and prolong the flowering period.

CONDITIONING AND VASE LIFE: 7 days.

USES: The bronzed bells of the later-flowering spires of *D. lanata* and *D. parviflora* are perfectly timed to pair with horizontal forms of achillea and soft grasses.

PROPAGATION: By seed in spring or autumn, most will flower in their second year.

Digitalis grandiflora with its buttery soft bells in a froth of white thalictrum.

Digitalis obscura 'Sunset' has burnished, wiry spires and is a good accent element.

Digitalis parviflora is the most vertical of the foxgloves, its bold shape works as a focal flower.

Echinacea purpurea
Coneflower

A classic of prairie-style planting, the striking daisy-shaped flowers are a valuable focal for late summer and early autumn. Originally they were just in shades of reddish-pink or white with pronounced orange cones, but recent breeding has expanded the colour range into a warmer palette of oranges, yellows and reds. I have found that these new offerings are very productive in their first year from seed but tend to be short-lived. Coneflowers dislike winter wet but do like moisture in the growing months.

Right: *Echinacea purpurea* 'White Swan' showing the three stages to maturity; the flower in the centre is ready to pick.

Below: *Echinacea purpurea* 'Magnus Superior' with spikes of *Persicaria amplexicaulis* 'Rosea'.

RECOMMENDED PLANTS:
E. purpurea 'Magnus Superior' – an improved form of a well-known magenta cultivar with horizontal petals, long-flowering. H 90cm (3ft)
E. purpurea 'White Swan' – understated greenish-white petals. H 70cm (2¼ft)

SPACING: 30cm (1ft) apart.

WHEN TO HARVEST: Once the petals have fully expanded.

CONDITIONING AND VASE LIFE: 10 days.

USES: A bold form which commands a starring role in a meadow-style arrangement with grasses and umbels.

PROPAGATION: Take basal cuttings or divide established clumps in spring. They can also be raised from seed, particularly the first-year-flowering varieties.

Echinops
Globe thistle

The perfectly spherical globed flower-heads are composed of hundreds of starry flowers, enjoyed by bees and butterflies from midsummer to early autumn. These large plants are rather coarse in the leaf and stem, but worth growing for their silvery or steely-blue textural orbs.

RECOMMENDED PLANTS:
E. bannaticus 'Star Frost' silver white, first year-flowering from seed. H 1.2m (4ft)
E. ritro 'Veitch's Blue' – rich indigo-blue flowers, slightly more refined and remains in a well-behaved clump. H 1m (3¼ft)

SPACING: 60cm (2ft) apart.

WHEN TO HARVEST: They can be picked fully open but I prefer the way they look when in spiny bud, this is also the right stage to harvest for drying.

CONDITIONING AND VASE LIFE: Remove leaves; 7–10 days.

USES: Their bold form underpins lighter, frothy flowers and they make an excellent dried flower.

PROPAGATION: By root cuttings in early winter, division in autumn or seed in spring.

Left: *Echinops ritro* 'Veitch's Blue'
Bottom: *Echinops bannaticus* 'Star Frost'

Eryngium
Sea holly

Striking thistle flowers in silvery sea greens, platinum and steely blues are produced on branching stems from midsummer to early autumn. Their sculptural form and metallic colours are always sought after by florists and they offer a rich nectar source to pollinators. Sea holly needs full sun to reach its best colour and well-drained soil to be reliably perennial.

RECOMMENDED PLANTS: *E. giganteum* 'Silver Ghost' – a ruff of showy platinum bracts, visciously prickly so handle with care. Short-lived but self seeds readily. H 75cm (2½ft)
E. planum 'Blue Glitter' – branched stems covered in a multitude of small thistles in a deep, metallic blue. A hardy, long lived variety. H 90cm (3ft)
E. planum 'White glitter' – glistening silver ivory flowers on stiffly upright branching stems. H 90cm (3ft)

SPACING: 30cm (1ft) apart.

CULTIVATION TIPS: Harvest all the stems of *E. planum* to encourage a second flush of flowers.

WHEN TO HARVEST: The tiny flowers which form the central cone should look tight, brightly coloured and not be giving off an unpleasant odour, which happens after pollination.

CONDITIONING AND VASE LIFE: 14 days

USES: The large, sculptural flowers of *E. giganteum* are eye-catching enough for focal status whilst *E. planum* are supporters with just two or three stems carrying a profusion of small thistles. I mostly use the silver varieties which blend across more colours. They dry well if picked at the same stage as for using fresh.

PROPAGATION: By fresh seed in autumn or by root cuttings in early winter.

Eryngium planum 'Blue Glitter' will give a second flush of flowers in early autumn if it is cut back promptly.

Euphorbia
Spurge

I was introduced to spurge many years ago by Sarah Raven – it is a mainstay of her cutting garden and floral brand. The acid-green flowering bracts are a jolt of bright contrast, which seem to work with any colour. They are fast-growing and productive plants flowering mid spring to early summer.

RECOMMENDED PLANTS:
E. amygdaloides var. *robbiae* – an evergreen variety which flowers in early spring. It is happy in dry shade, so can be tucked into hard-to-plant corners. H 60cm (2ft)
E. schillingii – a robust, tall form which flowers in midsummer with large, flat bracts. H 1m (3¼ft).

Euphorbia amygdaloides var. robbiae

SPACING: 30–50cm (12–19½in) apart.

WHEN TO HARVEST: Wait until the flowers are fully open and the stems feel ripe. *E. shillingii* can also be harvested for its seedheads and striking autumn colour. Wear gloves when handling as the milky sap can irritate the skin and eyes.

CONDITIONING AND VASE LIFE: Sear for 20 seconds; 7–10 days.

USES: The compact *E. amygdaloides* var. *robbiae* is a perky green companion to spring bulbs. It has rosettes of glossy dark green foliage which make an attractive collar in bouquets.

PROPAGATION: By division in spring or softwood cutting in early summer.

Foeniculum vulgare 'Purpureum'
Bronze fennel

I inherited this umbelliferous herb when we took on the land for our flower farm, which had previously been a market garden. It has proved its worth, so I have left it to continue self-seeding around the cutting beds. In spring it produces a haze of intensely bronze feathery foliage followed by sulphur-yellow umbels. H 1.5m (5ft)

RECOMMENDED PLANTS:
F. vulgare 'Giant Bronze' – a tall form with fine pewter colouring. H 1.8m (6ft)

SPACING: 45cm (17½in) apart.

WHEN TO HARVEST: In mid-spring for its foliage and midsummer through to early autumn for the flowers and seedheads.

CONDITIONING AND VASE LIFE: For the foliage, sear for 10 seconds. 5 days. The flowers are far more robust and can last for 14 days.

USES: The foliage adds texture and a welcome sour note to the sweetness of spring-flowering bulbs.

PROPAGATION: By seed sown in autumn or spring.

The feathery bronze foliage of *Foeniculum vulgare* 'Purpureum' provides a striking contrast in colour and texture to the sweet colours of spring bulbs.

Galega officinalis
Goat's rue

A robust bushy perennial, this is a mainstay for my large-scale midsummer arrangements. Its curvy branching stems are clothed with pinnate leaves and topped with pea-like flowers, resembling small, soft lilac lupins. Give it plenty of room and try to pick all the flowers to prevent it self-seeding, which it will do with gay abandon, sending down deep taproots. It prefers a sunny, open position. H 1.2m (4ft)

RECOMMENDED PLANT: *G. officinalis* 'Alba' – the white version.

CULTIVATION TIPS: It will need support, particularly in fertile soil where it will become lush and floppy.

WHEN TO HARVEST: Pick when the top of each raceme is still in bud. Conditioning and vase life: The stems are hollow, so benefit from being re-cut under water; 7–10 days.

USES: This is one of the few perennials I use as a framework element. In the summer months I find woody cuts can be a bit heavy-handed, as their full-size leaves can smother rather than frame the flowers.

PROPAGATION: Soak the hard coated seed for 12 hours and sow in early spring.

Galega officinalis

Gaura lindheimeri
White gaura

The tall, willowy stems are thronged with white flowers which open from pink buds – with their long stamens they look like fluttering clouds of butterflies as they waft in the breeze. The plants flower tirelessly from midsummer through to the first frosts. They like a sunny, dry position to be truly perennial and dislike winter wet, which can make them short-lived.
H 1.2m (4ft)

RECOMMENDED PLANTS:
G. lindheimeri 'Whirling Butterflies' – similar to the species but with a more upright, rigid habit which makes them easier for picking. H 65cm (2ft)

SPACING: 45cm (17½in) apart.

CULTIVATION TIPS: They will need support to stop them flopping over in heavy rain and winds.

WHEN TO HARVEST: In bud with just one or two flowers open on the stem.

CONDITIONING AND VASE LIFE: 5 days.

USES: I use the airy wands in a similar way to grasses to add movement and a light vertical accent.

PROPAGATION: By seed in early spring and they will flower in their first year.

Gaura lindheimeri 'Summer Breeze' has tall, pure white flowers with pink filaments.

Geum
Avens

This is a favourite perennial of many growers because of its dependability and timely profusion of flowers, just when the garden is experiencing a rather green gap in late spring. The flowers, borne on hairy stems from basal clumps of mid-green leaves, range from coppery apricots to fiery reds, golds and tangerine. There are many new hybrids with semi-double flowers and good stem length, which make the best cultivars for cutting. They enjoy a moisture-retentive soil in full sun.

RECOMMENDED PLANTS: For cutting, the cocktail and tempest series are worth exploring.

G. 'Bell Bank' – muted coral pink, semi-double flower. H 45cm (17½in)

G. 'Mai Tai' – peachy-pink, semi-double flowers with striking burgundy sepals and stems. H 45cm (17½in)

G. 'Poco' – parent to many of the new hybrids, with burgundy stems and buds and golden flowers. H 45cm (17½in)

G. SCARLET TEMPEST – large fiery scarlet flowers produced in two good flushes in late spring and again in late summer. H 50cm (19½in)

G. 'Totally Tangerine' – the longest stem length and flowering period. Warm orange flowers. H 60cm (2ft)

SPACING: 45cm (17½in) apart.

WHEN TO HARVEST: From late spring to early summer.

CONDITIONING AND VASE LIFE: Sear for 10 seconds. 7 days; the buds will open in the vase and are often a lighter shade, creating a two-toned effect.

USES: Their slender stems and small, slightly nodding flowers make a good accent element in a mixed arrangement. They lighten heavier, blowsier blooms and add enlivening flecks of colour.

PROPAGATION: By summer division.

Below: The beautifully coloured *Geum* 'Mai Tai' is relatively short but with regular watering the stems can be encouraged to reach a cut-worthy length.

Opposite, left to right: *Geum* 'Scarlet Tempest'; a mix of 'Poco', 'Mai Tai' and 'Totally Tangerine'; *Geum* 'Totally Tangerine' growing among cow parsley, inspiration for the vase.

Gillenia trifoliata
Bowman's root

This plant is one of my favourites, which I have to confess I find hard to pick partly because I like it so much but also because it is a slow grower, taking up to four years to reach its full size. It has a refined delicacy, with deep russet-coloured wiry stems bedecked with clouds of white starry flowers in early summer. In autumn its leaves turn to glowing reds and oranges. Position in full sun or part shade in a moisture-retentive soil. H 75cm (2½ft)

SPACING: 30cm (1ft) apart.

WHEN TO HARVEST: As soon as the flowers begin to open and again in the autumn for its foliage.

CONDITIONING AND VASE LIFE: 5 days.

USES: Retain its light, airy structure by keeping it simple; it works beautifully arranged with roses.

PROPAGATION: By division in early spring or by seed sown in the autumn outdoors, to germinate the following year.

Gillenia trifoliata

Helleborus × hybridus
Hellebore

Left: *H. × hybridus* 'Harvington Picotee'; *H. × hybridus* 'Harvington Shades of Night'

Below: *H. × hybridus* 'Double Cream Speckled'

One of the oldest inhabitants of our garden, hellebores are the first cut flowers of the season, providing sumptuous blooms in late winter through to a muted, earthier version in mid-spring. You can easily become a hellebore collector, with single and double forms spanning the colour spectrum including soft apricots, chartreuse greens and deep slate purples. They enjoy dappled shade, shelter and a rich, preferably moisture-retentive soil. We have created a microclimate for ours at the base of a guelder rose hedge. The plants are slow to bulk up, but they are long-lived. H 45cm (17½in).

RECOMMENDED PLANTS: I acquired my collection of Harvington cultivars from nurseryman and life-long hellebore breeder Hugh Nunn. His dedicated and methodical hybridizing has produced flower colours with real depth and clarity.

SPACING: 45cm (17½in) apart.

WHEN TO HARVEST: Hellebores are notorious for wilting quickly after being cut, and even with searing will last only a couple of days. I still cannot resist bringing them into the house in February with snowdrops, for a much-needed lift. If that feels a little wasteful and you would prefer

more longevity, wait for their stamens to drop and seedpods to swell.

CONDITIONING AND VASE LIFE: The stems benefit from being seared in 5cm of boiling water for about 30 seconds. 3 days if cut before seed capsules form, 2 weeks if after.

USES: The ripened stems make the perfect supporting flower to spring bulbs, a practical option when their vase life is at its longest. They are the perfect understated companion to flamboyant tulips. Give them plenty of space in a wide-mouthed vessel so that their graceful arching stems and nodding heads can be appreciated.

PROPAGATION: Sow fresh seed in summer and place outdoors in a shady cold frame. Germination normally occurs the following winter.

HELLEBORE KEY

1 *H. × hybridus* 'Harvington Double Cream Speckled'
2 *H. × hybridus* 'Harvington Shades of Night'
3 *H. × hybridus* 'Harvington Picotee'
4 *H. × hybridus* 'Harvington Double Pink'
5 *H. × hybridus* 'Harvington Single White'
6 *H. × hybridus* 'Harvington Single Red'
7 *H. × hybridus* 'Harvington Double White'
8 *H. × hybridus* 'Harvington Double Apricot'
9 *H. × hybridus* 'Harvington Double Red'
10 *H. × hybridus* 'Harvington Single Apricot'
11 *H. × hybridus* 'Harvington Single Yellow'

Hylotelephium
Stonecrop

This sturdy, succulent plant with its broad domed heads can be a bit clumpy to use unless it has experienced the 'Chelsea chop'. By cutting it back by a third in late spring it will produce an abundance of smaller flowers which are far more appropriate for their role as a supporting element. This technique also delays their flowering until early autumn, when they are even more appreciated by the bees. They thrive in poor soil with good drainage and full sun.

RECOMMENDED PLANTS:
H. 'Matrona' – pewter leaves with purple stems and rose-pink flowers, strong, upright stems. H 60cm (2ft)
H. spectabile 'Iceberg' – pale green buds open to greenish-white starry flowers. H 40cm (15½in)

SPACING: 45cm (17½in) apart.

WHEN TO HARVEST: When a few of the star-shaped flowers have opened.

CONDITIONING AND VASE LIFE: 14 days.

USES: I find the flowers easier to use in tight bud when their broccoli-like texture offers a good contrast to dahlias. They hold well out of water so are useful for installation work.

PROPAGATION: By division in autumn or spring.

Hylotelephium 'Matrona' in tight bud at the 'broccoli stage' which is when I find it most useful as a textural, suppporting flower.

Iris germanica
bearded iris

The most indulged of perennial cut flowers, these prima donnas demand perfect weather conditions, their own space and only perform for a fleeting but glorious two weeks. Each time I see their petals puckered by rain, ravaged by slugs or torn by windy weather I wonder why I bother but when they are revelling in the sunshine in all their statuesque glory all is forgiven. Apart from their appearance they do have some practical benefits – their flowering time bridges the gap in focal flowers between late spring and early summer and after an initial investment they bulk up quickly coming in every possible colour, many with contrasting standard and fall colours.

RECOMMENDED PLANTS: There are hundreds of hybrids to choose from, if you like lots of ruffle and flounce look at the modern hybrids. For something more understated, the Benton Irises bred by Cedric Morris are worth exploring.

To prolong their short flowering season this selection offers a wide range of bloom times.

'June Prom' – an intermediate with short standards and broad falls, in the palest blue overlaid with dull green veining. H 45cm (17½in)
'Pink Charm' – peachy-pink with a bold tangerine beard. Generous and scented. H 60cm (2ft)
'Benton Susan' – my personal favourite for its buff colouring, simple form and abundant tall flowering stems. H 1m (3¼ft)
'Benton Deirdre' – a rose pink, subtle but intriguing. H 1m (3¼ft)
'Carnaby' – apricot standards with large rosy purple falls. H 80cm (2½ft)
'Butterscotch Kiss' – very large flowers in a delicious butterscotch yellow. H 90cm (3ft)

'Foggy Dew' – a healthy, vigorous old variety with exquisite colouring to rival any modern hybrid, cream washed with pale lavender. H 65cm (2ft)
'Beverley Sills' – a soft peach pink, one of the most reliable in this colour. H 75cm (2½ft)
'Jane Phillips' – this classic iris is deservedly one of the most popular varieties, large pale blue, highly scented flowers. H 80cm (2¾ft)
'Mur du Sud' – very large violet purple flowers, with a cornflower-blue beard, ruffled and abundant. H 80cm (2¾ft)

SPACING: Plant at 45cm (17½in) apart to ensure good airflow to prevent leaf spot.

CULTIVATION TIPS: Plant rhizomes on the surface of the soil with the fan to the north, so that it bakes in the sun. We plant ours on ridges to improve drainage

WHEN TO HARVEST: Iris petals are fragile and can bruise or tear very easily, so try and pick when they are in bud with the primary flower showing good colour and starting to unfurl.

CONDITIONING AND VASE LIFE: Each flower will last for 3 days, remove the spent flowers to encourage the next one down the stem to open. 7-10 days.

USES: Flowering time coincides with fellow cottage garden favourites like foxgloves and sweet rocket. Bentons blend well in meadow-style arrangements with buttercups and astrantia.

PROPAGATION: To keep them flowering freely irises should be divided every three years.

'Benton Susan'

'Carnaby'

'Jane Phillips'

'Pink Charm'

'June Prom'

'Mur du Sud'

'Beverley Sills'

'Foggy Dew'

Lamprocapnos spectabilis (syn. *Dicentra spectabilis*)
Bleeding heart

One of our first perennials to flower in mid-spring, the clumps of fresh green foliage producing elegantly arching sprays of dangling heart-shaped flowers. This woodland plant is happiest in part shade and moist soil. To emulate these conditions we grow it between rows of shrubs with plenty of irrigation, which also protects it from wind and damaging late frosts. H 45cm (17½in)

RECOMMENDED PLANTS: *Lamprocapnos spectabilis* 'Alba', a stylish pure white cultivar.

SPACING: 45cm (17½in) apart.

WHEN TO HARVEST: Once half the hearts have peeled open, revealing their white centres.

Lamprocaprios spectabilis, both the flowers and foliage are a valuable mid-spring supporting element.

CONDITIONING AND VASE LIFE: 7–10 days.

USES: An accent element whose arching shapes and ferny foliage are a counterpoint to tulips and ranunculus. The rose-pink colour makes a good clash with many of the spring bulbs such as coral tulips and orange crown imperial fritillary.

PROPAGATION: From seed after a chilling period in the refrigerator.

Leucanthemum × superbum
Shasta daisies

This group of large, brilliant white daisies look like tamed versions of wild ox-eyes. I prefer the single forms that introduce a meadow feel in midsummer. They also tend to be the most reliable and long-lived. Some cultivars are more attention-seeking, such as the shaggy doubles and anemone-centred cultivars. They do best in full sun and moist soil.

RECOMMENDED PLANTS:
L. × superbum 'Aglaia' – almost fully double at first, but opens to show a golden-yellow eye. H 60cm (2ft)
L. × superbum 'Becky' – an abundance of single flowers on tall, sturdy stems from mid to late summer. H 1m (3¼ft)
L. × superbum 'T. E. Killin' – large anemone-centred flowers with a double layer of petals. H 1m (3¼ft)

SPACING: 30cm (1ft) apart.

WHEN TO HARVEST: When the petals, also known as rays, have opened but the central eye is tight.

CONDITIONING AND VASE LIFE: 7–10 days.

USES: As a focal flower, they add a cheerful, uplifting feel to an arrangement.

PROPAGATION: By division in early spring or late summer every 2-3 years to retain their flowering potential.

Leucanthemum × superbum 'Becky' a simple single form that brings a wild-flower feel to an arrangement.

Limonium tataricum
Statice

This is one of my best discoveries from the perennial seed suppliers Jelitto. It far surpassed my expectations gleaned from the catalogue description and has become my go-to substitute for gypsophila, which does not grow well enough in our climate. The plants are highly productive, yielding an abundant crop of silvery-white clusters of flowers on densely branched stems. When we harvest these in midsummer they are hung in our barn to dry for a couple of weeks and then become a staple supporting flower for the rest of the season. They have one drawback – if the flowers get wet they smell something akin to rotting flesh. These plants need free-draining soil in full sun to thrive. H 45cm (17½in)

RECOMMENDED PLANTS:
L. latifolium – sea lavender, with large, airy sprays of tiny, pale lavender flowers. I tend to use this fresh rather than dried. H 65cm (2ft)

SPACING: 30cm (1ft) apart.

WHEN TO HARVEST: Pick when the flowers have turned from pink to white and are fully open.

CONDITIONING AND VASE LIFE: It lasts for 14 days as a fresh cut flower and dries quickly when hung upside down.

USES: A frothy supporting flower which has a prolonged season because it dries so well. A mainstay for hanging installations and Christmas wreaths.

PROPAGATION: By seed in spring, it will flower in its second year.

Left: *Limonium tataricum*
Right: *Limonium latifolium*

Linaria purpurea
Toadflax

Slender, delicate spires of shell-pink flowers resembling small snapdragons appear from early to late summer. It is easy to grow and will flower prolifically in a sunny spot with well-drained soil. H 90cm (3ft)

RECOMMENDED PLANTS: *L.* 'Peachy' – a new Linaria hybrid with creamy peach flowers. H 1m (3¼ft)

SPACING: 30cm (1ft) apart.

CULTIVATION TIPS: Cut back in early spring and after first flush to stimulate further flowering. In richer soils the plants might require staking.

WHEN TO HARVEST: When the bottom half of the florets are open.

CONDITIONING AND VASE LIFE: 14 days.

USES: A dainty spire-shaped supporting flower.

PROPAGATION: By seed in autumn or spring and it will flower in its first year.

Linaria purpurea 'Canon Went'

Lysimachia clethroides
Gooseneck loosestrife

These plants are vigorous and often classed as a thug in the garden, but to a flower farmer that just means they are very productive. The elegantly shaped spikes of small, white, starry flowers come into flower in midsummer. The leaves turn a rich red in the autumn. It does need a rich, moist soil if it is to conquer a border. H 80cm (2¾ft)

RECOMMENDED PLANTS: *L. ephemerum*, the willow-leaved loosestrife, has soft, grey-green foliage with tall, slender spires of starry white flowers with pink stamens. These are followed by sculptural seedheads. It is a very productive plant, but it does tend to run out of steam after about four years. H 1m (3¼ft)

SPACING: 45cm (17½in) apart.

WHEN TO HARVEST: Once the bottom third of the florets are open.

CONDITIONING AND VASE LIFE: 10 days.

USES: The kinked flowers of *L. clethroides* convey the idea of movement in arrangements, especially when used in groups facing in the same direction.

PROPAGATION: Lift and divide *L. clethroides* every 3 years to stop it becoming congested and smaller-flowered. Sow *L. ephemerum* seed in early spring.

Above: *Lysimachia ephemerum* at different stages of flowering, the picture on the right shows it at the right stage for harvesting.

Opposite page: *Lysimachia clethroides* clearly showing why it's common name is gooseneck.

Macleaya microcarpa 'Spetchley Ruby'
Plume poppy

I grow this handsome plant for its bold foliage and plumes of flower. The lobed greyish-green leaves are carried on 20cm (8in) long petioles, which means they have enough stem length to use on their own. The towering stems are topped by large panicles of feathery terracotta flowers, which turn to ruby-red seedheads by late summer. Be warned it is a notorious spreader, quickly outgrowing its space by shallow running roots. It likes rich, moist soil and full sun. H 1.8m (6ft)

Right: *Macleaya microcarpa* 'Spetchley Ruby'

RECOMMENDED PLANTS: *M. cordata* – creamy-buff flowers, less invasive than *M. microcarpa*. H 2m (6½ft)

SPACING: 1m (3¼ft) apart.

WHEN TO HARVEST: When all the flowers have opened. Beware of the sap – it is not toxic but does stain.

CONDITIONING AND VASE LIFE: Sear both flowering stems and leaves for 20 seconds; 10 days.

USES: The fig-like leaves can act as a collar to soften the rim of a vase, while the flower plumes or seedheads can be used tucked in as a textural supporting flower or tall as an airy accent.

PROPAGATION: By division in spring or autumn or by root cuttings in winter.

Mentha
Mint

I discovered the benefits of mint as a cut foliage after an extremely harsh winter had killed off all of my newly planted shrubs. In a panic I rushed out and bought a tray of apple mint plug plants. They grew quickly and I was rewarded with an abundance of harvestable stems just a few months after planting.

RECOMMENDED PLANTS: We grow a range of mint for a succession of flowers and variety of scent and leaf colour. If you have room for only one, *M. suaveolens* (apple mint) is a good choice, it has robust, long stems and is early into leaf and flower. H 1m (3¼ft)

M. longifolia (buddleia mint) – tall, branching and silver leaved. H 90cm (3ft)
M. × citrata 'Lavender' (lavender mint) deep green flushed purple. H 80cm (2¾ft)
M. spicata var. *crispa* 'Moroccan' (Moroccan mint) – bright green with white flowers. H 60cm (2ft)
M. 'Strawberry Mint' – small grey-green leaves. H 40cm (15½in)
M. suaveolens 'Variegata' (pineapple mint) – variegated and late to flower. H 60cm (2ft)

SPACING: 40cm (15½in) apart.

CULTIVATION TIPS: Harvesting the stems regularly keeps the plants in check and prevents them taking over.

WHEN TO HARVEST: The stems are best picked from midsummer onwards when they have ripened and have some woody growth – ideally just before or during flowering.

CONDITIONING AND VASE LIFE: Softer foliage will need an overnight condition. They have a surprisingly long vase life of up to 2 weeks and even produce roots if they are left long enough.

USES: All the mints are supporting foliage or flowers. I mainly use them for hand-tied bouquets, where their straight stems and scented foliage are most appreciated.

PROPAGATION: To maintain vigour and long lush stems, lift and divide every three years and move to a new area prepared with plenty of organic matter.

Top: *Mentha suaveolens*

Middle: *Mentha spicata* var. *crispa* 'Moroccan'

Bottom: By growing a number of cultivars we have a long succession of flower spikes from our mint row.

Nepeta nuda
Naked catmint

I fell for this upright catmint on a visit to Beth Chatto's garden in early summer when it was in full soft flower and absolutely smothered in bees. It has a clump-forming habit, aromatic foliage and tall, candelabra spires of grey-lavender flowers, which create a subtle, misty effect. It likes full sun and well-drained soil. H 1m (3¼ft)

Nepeta nuda 'Romany Dusk' the flowering stems have a ghostly, transparent appearance which can be used as a subtle foil for more eye-popping colours.

RECOMMENDED PLANTS: *N. nuda* 'Romany Dusk' – a suave form with sultry dark stems contrasting with pale, lilac flowers. The tall stems are self-supporting and if cut back will flower again in the autumn. H 1.5m (5ft)

SPACING: 30cm (1ft) apart.

WHEN TO HARVEST: When half the flowers on the stem are open.

CONDITIONING AND VASE LIFE: 7 days.

USES: As a delicate, ghostly vertical accent.

PROPAGATION: By basal cuttings in spring.

Origanum vulgare subsp. *hirtum*
Greek oregano

This culinary herb is one of our most useful supporting flowers. From midsummer it produces mounds of fragrant white and blush-pink flowers, which are mobbed by bees and butterflies. The harvest period goes on into late summer, when it produces fluffy, green seedheads. It is a first-year-flowering perennial which is most productive in the second year. Unsurprisingly given its name, it likes hot dry weather. H 45cm (17½in)

RECOMMENDED PLANTS:
O. laevigatum 'Herrenhausen' – an ornamental, mauve-pink, later-flowering form. H 60cm (2ft)

SPACING: 30cm (1ft) apart.

WHEN TO HARVEST: It can be picked when in bud, in full flower and as seedheads.

CONDITIONING AND VASE LIFE: 7–10 days.

USES: A staple for bouquet work, the clusters of small flowers and leaves form a scented backdrop for other flowers with more defined form and colour.

PROPAGATION: By seed in spring or autumn. Sow annually to ensure the continuity of productive plants.

Origanum vulgare subsp. *hirtum* is one of my most versatile summer supporting flowers, its neutral colouring and aromatic fragrance works well in bouquets and table centrepieces.

Paeonia
Peony

Growing peonies for cutting always feels rather decadent, as it takes precious space and time to bring these luscious beauties to maturity. The reward for giving them a prime spot and waiting for three years to pick them is a glorious but fleeting two to three weeks of fragrant, blowsy heaven. On the plus side they are very long-lived plants and are also incredibly hardy, relishing a cold winter and needing very little attention considering the extravagance of their blooms. They do best in well-drained soil with full sun and should not be planted too deeply, with the buds (known as eyes) no more than 2.5cm (1in) below the surface. For the first two years just deadhead the flowers – it is important not to pick the stems as the crowns need to bulk up and mature. We grow the herbaceous type of peonies for cutting – *P. lactiflora* – which are mostly whites, creams and pinks and include many of the full double forms. The other type are hybrids with *P. lactiflora* in their breeding, which are generally single or semi-double forms and come in a wider colour palette including corals and yellows. They are also more robust and generally earlier to flower, which is useful for filling the late spring gap in focal flowers. H 90cm (3ft)

RECOMMENDED PLANTS: To make the most of their short season, select a combination of early, mid and late season cultivars, which will flower from late spring to midsummer.

P. 'Buckeye Belle' – hybrid, with glossy, rich deep red semi-double with striking golden stamens. Early.

P. 'Coral Charm' – hybrid, with large deeply cupped semi-double coral that fades to apricot. Early.

P. 'Cytherea' – hybrid, with large bowl-shaped semi-double magenta pink with gold stamens.

P. 'Etched Salmon' – hybrid, with shallow domed cups of salmon-pink. Mid.

P. lactiflora 'Duchesse de Nemours' – classic, ivory, highly fragrant double with creamy centres. Mid.

P. lactiflora 'Elsa Sass' – pure white, shallow bowl. Late.

P. lactiflora 'Festiva Maxima' – double, creamy white with raspberry flecks in centres. Early.

P. lactiflora 'Gardenia' – one of the most sweet-scented peonies, shaped like a cabbage rose, double white with blush pink tints. Mid.

P. lactiflora 'Kansas' – frilly domes of dark magenta. Mid.

P. lactiflora 'Sarah Bernhardt' – one of the most recognizable peonies, pale powder pink, fluffy domes, very productive and reliable. Late.

P. 'Soft Salmon Saucer' – hybrid, small single, soft-pink goblet-shaped. Early.

SPACING: 80cm–1m (2¾– 3¼ft) apart; they need plenty of space to allow good airflow and prevent botrytis, a common problem caused by wet weather.

Opposite page left to right: *Peony* 'Buckeye Belle', *P. lactiflora* 'Kansas'

Below: *Peony lactiflora* 'Sarah Bernhardt'

CULTIVATION TIPS: In the spring mulch very lightly – do not bury them as this will prevent them from flowering properly. Support with netting as the flowerheads can get very weighty. Cut back promptly in autumn and top-dress with a sprinkle of bonemeal.

WHEN TO HARVEST: At the 'marshmallow' stage, which means in bud but when gently squeezed it feels soft and squidgy. Only harvest a third of the flowers from a plant and be mindful of where you cut; leave at least two sets of leaves on the stem or you will deplete the plant's energy reserves.

CONDITIONING AND VASE LIFE: Keep the vase topped up, as peonies are thirsty flowers; 7–10 days. White and pink varieties tend to have the longest vase life.

USES: The enormous, overblown blooms of the double peonies are hard to arrange, as too many in a bouquet can look rather 'roundy moundy'. The semi-doubles and singles are much easier to blend with other early summer flowers. I like to combine them with smaller flowers that have a similar composition of petals and stamens, such as poppies and buttercups. Spires of foxgloves are a good contrast to break up their large bowl-shapes.

PROPAGATION: If you are planning on going big with peonies it is much cheaper to buy bare-root stock during the dormant season. Established clumps that are eight years or older can be divided in the autumn once the leaves have died back. Each root division must have at least three eyes.

It is sunrise in early summer and we wait for the dew-drenched peony buds to dry before harvesting them at the marshmallow stage.

Penstemon barbatus 'Jingle Bells'
Beard tongue

I gravitate towards the smaller-flowered cultivars of *Penstemon* as they suit my naturalistic style, are hardier and seem to hold better once cut. From mid to late summer, 'Jingle Bells' has long, graceful flower spikes that carry clusters of slender coral-red tubular bells all the way along the stems. It requires full sun and well-drained soil. H 90cm (3ft)

RECOMMENDED PLANTS:
P. digitalis 'Husker Red' – the best variety for vase life and the first to flower in early summer. A stylish cut flower with burgundy stems and delicate tubular mother of pearl flowers, followed by attractive seedheads. H 50cm (19½in)

SPACING: 30cm (1ft) apart.

WHEN TO HARVEST: When half the flowers on the stem are open.

CONDITIONING AND VASE LIFE: Sear. 5–7 days.

USES: A brilliant willowy accent flower which adds splashes of vivid colour, without overwhelming an arrangement.

PROPAGATION: Easy from seed sown in early spring.

Left: *Penstemon digitalis* 'Husker Red'
Right: *Penstemon barbatus* 'Jingle Bells'

Persicaria alpina
Alpine knotweed

By far the largest perennial I grow, it towers above me by midsummer when its race to the sky erupts into creamy foaming panicles resembling giant astilbe flowers. I was advised by the nursery to give it plenty of space and not to order too many. I bought ten plants which is more than enough for my needs as a professional grower. It is tough, self-supporting and will create a fast-growing shelter belt for less self-sufficient plants. Position in full sun or light shade; it will do better in moist soil and can cope with waterlogging. H 2m (6½ft)

SPACING: 1m (3¼ft) apart.

WHEN TO HARVEST: The tiny flowers on the panicles need to be open and the stems should feel firm and ripe. It can also be harvested in late summer when the flowers have aged to a bronzy pink.

CONDITIONING AND VASE LIFE: Cut hollow stems under hand-hot water and leave to condition overnight. 5 days.

USES: Branching stems can be used as a framework element for large-scale arrangements. Smaller side branches make good supporting flowers.

PROPAGATION: By division in early spring.

Persicaria alpina is a useful large-scale supporting flower in early summer and the sheer volume of material the plants produce is a gift if you are growing for weddings.

Phlox
Phlox

The sweet, peppery scent of phlox is so evocative of balmy summer days. It might not be the most elegant flower with its rather unshapely dense panicles, but it is worth growing for its fragrance and gap-filling flowering time between mid and late summer. It is at its best in light shade and a moisture-retentive soil.

RECOMMENDED PLANTS:
P. × arendsii 'Hesperis' – looking rather like its namesake sweet rocket, with small lilac-pink flowers. H 80cm (2¾ft)
P. × arendsii 'Utopia' – early-flowering, with large, open, airy panicles of pale lilac-pink. Very fragrant. H 1.2m (4ft)
P. paniculata 'Blue Paradise' – a colour-shifter that will appear a purple-pink when warm and a purple-blue when cooler. H 80cm (2¾ft)
P. paniculata 'Bright Eyes' – not for the faint-hearted, this vibrant pink phlox with darker pink eyes is highly productive and mildew-resistant. H 80cm (2¾ft)
P. paniculata 'Franz Schubert' – my favourite, a pearly lilac with lighter centres and edges. H 80cm (2¾ft)

P. paniculata 'Mount Fuji' – the last to flower, with small, pure white blooms in narrow upright clusters, good for bouquets. H 1m (3¼ft)

SPACING: 45cm (17½in) apart.

CULTIVATION TIPS: To stagger flowering time and produce multi-headed stems of smaller flowers, perform the Chelsea chop on some of the plants in late spring.

WHEN TO HARVEST: Once half the florets are open.

CONDITIONING AND VASE LIFE: Shake flowers to dislodge any ageing florets and make room for buds to open. 10 days.

USES: Their irregular rather 'blobby' shape means they are best used as a supporting flower between more defined shapes where they add volume and room-filling fragrance.

PROPAGATION: By division every 3 years to avoid congestion and resulting mildew. To avoid the spread of eelworm by root cuttings in early winter.

Top: *Phlox paniculata* 'Franz Schubert'

Middle: *Phlox paniculata* 'Mount Fuji'

Bottom: *Phlox × arendsii* has large cool pink flowers which blend well with blues and lilacs.

Physostegia virginiana 'Vivid'
Obedience plant

The small lavender-pink tubular flowers of this plant emerge on all four sides of square-stemmed spires. The individual florets stay put once placed, hence its common name. It is a strong grower that will happily produce armfuls of snapdragon-like flowers in late summer just as there is a lull in the spire form in the rest of the garden. The foliage and seedheads take on an attractive burgundy hue after flowering, which extends the harvest period. It is a tough, easy-to-grow plant with a good sturdy habit, which means it does not require staking. Position in full sun or part shade in moist, well-drained soil. H 80cm (2¾ft)

RECOMMENDED PLANTS:
P. virginiana 'Miss Manners' – a white-flowering form. H 1m (3¼ft)

SPACING: 30cm (1ft) apart.

WHEN TO HARVEST: Once a couple of rows of florets are open at the base of the spire; at this stage they will continue to open in the vase.

CONDITIONING AND VASE LIFE: 10–14 days.

USES: A good supporting flower with dahlias. The seedheads dry well.

PROPAGATION: By division in spring, every 3 years to retain flower size and stem length.

Physostegia virginiana 'Vivid' – the small trumpet flowers are held on elegant upright spires.

Polemonium 'Lambrook Mauve'
Jacob's ladder

This is one of the loveliest late spring-flowering perennials and a very welcome supporting flower during a lean time for this element. Scented sprays of pale mauve flowers are produced from a mound of ferny foliage. For maximum stem length, grow in partial shade and moist soil. H 30-45cm (12–15½in)

SPACING: 30cm (1ft) apart.

RECOMMENDED PLANTS:
P. 'Sonia's Bluebell' – violet-scented, wedgewood-blue flowers are produced from early summer over a long flowering period. I was given this wonderful plant by a plantswoman who grows it at the base of her polytunnel so that it benefits from the run off. H 50cm (19½in)
P. carneum 'Apricot Delight' has flowers in a soft, pinky-apricot which is a unique colour for the genus. H 40cm (15½in)

WHEN TO HARVEST: When one third to half of the flowers are open.

CONDITIONING AND VASE LIFE: As individual flowers fade, more will open in the vase in a lighter shade; 7–10 days.

USES: Its cottage-garden character makes it the perfect supporting flower in relaxed, 'just picked' arrangements.

PROPAGATION: By division in autumn.

Polemonium 'Lambrook Mauve', the dainty clusters of soft mauve flowers and ferny foliage can hold their own in a vase or look pretty in a jumbled cottage garden posy.

Polygonatum × hybridum
Solomon's seal

A woodlander that produces clumps of gracefully arching stems of oval, pleated alternate leaves in late spring. Suspended beneath the leaf axils are clusters of waxy bell-shaped flowers, which are creamy with green tips. These are followed by deep-blue berries in the autumn. If you can provide a shady, moist position the plants can reach a height of 90cm (3ft). Our farm is a bit short on moist shade so we have created a bed along the edge of our polytunnel which benefits from all the rain run-off.

RECOMMENDED PLANTS:
P. multiflorum is slightly shorter and more upright.

Polygonatum × hybridum

SPACING: 30cm (1ft) apart.

WHEN TO HARVEST: Cut the stems at ground level when half of the flowers are open. Pick again in the autumn for the striking berries.

CONDITIONING AND VASE LIFE: 7–10 days.

USES: A bold, architectural stem which is best used in large arrangements where it can assume the same stance as in the border.

PROPAGATION: Divide in early spring before growth begins, ensuring each piece of rhizome has a terminal bud.

Pulmonaria OPAL
Lungwort

Lungworts are a close second to hellebores for the first perennials to pick each year on our farm. I can overlook their diminutive stature because of their early-spring flowering and old-fashioned charm. The cowslip-like flowers are opalescent, changing from pink in bud to an ice blue as they open. They are accompanied by low-growing silver spotted foliage. H 35cm (13½in)

RECOMMENDED PLANTS:
'Blue Ensign' – electric-blue flowers. H 45cm (17½in)

SPACING: 30cm (1ft) apart.

WHEN TO HARVEST: When about half the flowers are open.

CONDITIONING AND VASE LIFE: Sear for 10 seconds. 7 days.

USES: I like to pick a handful of stems to display in a small jug on my desk, so that I can appreciate the delicacy of their flowers up close.

Pulmonaria OPAL

Ranunculus acris 'Citrinus'
Meadow buttercup

Our native meadow buttercup grows with lush abundance in the water meadows next to the farm and has always been one of my favourite flowers to forage in late spring. Recently I discovered this refined version. *R. a.* 'Citrinus' produces floating clouds of shimmering flowers on fine branching stems. Its pale lemon, shiny petals create little flecks of light through arrangements. It prefers sun and moist soil. Height 45cm (17½in).

RECOMMENDED PLANTS: *R. acris* 'Stevenii' is a giant form with semi-double flowers on tall stems. H 1m (3¼ft).

SPACING: 30cm (1ft) apart.

WHEN TO HARVEST: Pick when half the flowers on a stem are open.

CONDITIONING AND VASE LIFE: Sear for 10 seconds. 7 days.

USES: It looks most at home when used in a meadow-style arrangement with early-summer hardy annuals such as cornflowers and white lace flower.

PROPAGATION: Summer division is a reliable way to bulk up your stock. Otherwise you can grow from seed but it must be sown fresh for it to germinate reliably.

Ranunculus acris 'Citrinus'

Rudbeckia triloba 'Prairie Glow'
Brown-eyed Susan

I had been searching for a brown-eyed Susan that I liked for sometime before I chanced upon this one in the Jelitto seed catalogue. The small black-eyed daisies have striking, burnt orange petals with yellow tips. H 1.5m (5ft).

RECOMMENDED PLANTS: *R. triloba* – the species is also worth trying, because of the daintiness of its flowers and their airy spacing, the golden-yellow sprays are less dominating in a display. H 1m (3¼ft)

SPACING: 30cm (1ft) apart.

CULTIVATION TIPS: Plants will need support as they can get top-heavy when in flower.

WHEN TO HARVEST: Early autumn when the flowers are fully open but the central cone is still tight.

CONDITIONING AND VASE LIFE: 7–10 days. Add a drop of bleach to the water to keep the water clear as the stems tend to make it murky.

USES: The profusion of flowers on each tall, branching stem creates airy sprays which make it an ideal supporting flower from late summer to mid-autumn. I like to pair it with grasses for a prairie-style look.

PROPAGATION: Sow in late winter for flowers by late summer. Sadly it is not reliably hardy, so treat it as a short-lived perennial and sow every year.

Rudbeckia triloba 'Prairie Glow'

Salvia × sylvestris 'Lye End'
Wood sage

I have trialled a few salvias over the years and have found that this one has all the right attributes for cutting. It is a strong grower, coming back year after year, and a profuse bloomer, with a long flowering period from mid to late summer. It has branched, upright spikes in lavender blue. It requires full sun and well-drained soil. H 70cm (2¼ft).

RECOMMENDED PLANTS:
S. nemorosa 'Amethyst' – slender spires of lilac-purple, a long flowering period. H 60cm (2ft)
S. × sylvestris 'Dear Anja' – a Piet Oudolf selection with striking purple stems densely packed with vibrant blue flowers. H 80cm (2¾ft).

SPACING: 30cm (1ft) apart.

WHEN TO HARVEST: The spikes can be picked when at least half the flowers have opened.

CONDITIONING AND VASE LIFE: 7 days.

USES: The fine, richly coloured spikes work well with other flowers that pick out their colours, including amsonias and *Papaver rhoeas* 'Amazing Grey' poppies.

PROPAGATION: Basal cuttings in early spring or semi-ripe cuttings in late summer.

Below left: *Salvia nemorosa* 'Amethyst'
Below right: *Salvia × sylvestris* 'Lye End'

Sanguisorba
Burnet

A few years back, in a fit of enthusiasm for this fashionable genus, I bought a good ten cultivars. I then lost most of the labels and realized they all look pretty similar and it was impossible to work out which was which. The benefit of having such a selection is that it prolongs their flowering season from late spring to early autumn. During this acute sanguisorba phase I used them in virtually everything I made, smitten with the generous swarms of burgundy bobbles on wiry stems. They are easy-to-grow stalwarts, clumping up quickly – all they require is full sun and a moisture-retentive soil, otherwise sulking and mildew may ensue.

RECOMMENDED PLANTS:
S. 'Cangshan Cranberry' is a late-summer variety with long-lasting, deep red, erect flowers on tall stems. H 1.5-1.8m (5–6ft)

Top: *Sanguisorba* 'Cangshan Cranberry'
Bottom: *Sanguisorba menziesii*

S. menziesii is the earliest to flower in late spring. It also sports the largest flower-heads in a deep maroon – if there is plenty of moisture they may be up to 7cm long. H 70cm (2¼ft)
S. officinalis is a good one to start with, as it germinates easily from seed and will produce an abundance of stems for cutting from midsummer. H 1.2m (4ft)
S. tenuifolia var. *alba* 'Korean Snow' is a tall, elegant, white form. H 1.5m (5ft)

SPACING: 45cm (17½in) apart.

WHEN TO HARVEST: The bobble-like flowers should be tight and the stems green and firm.

CONDITIONING AND VASE LIFE: 7–10 days.

USES: They have the magic touch when it comes to adding air and movement to arrangements.

PROPAGATION: Divide clumps in spring or autumn. *S. officinalis* is easy from seed.

Scabiosa caucasica 'Perfecta Blue'
Scabious

One of my most desirable plants for both customers and pollinators, it seems to encapsulate 'English country garden' with the soft lavender-blue colouring and daisy shape of the flowers. It is a first-year-flowering perennial, which is easy from seed but will be short-lived if the soil gets waterlogged in the winter. If the plants are picked and deadheaded regularly they can be productive for three months, particularly in their second year. Position in an open, sunny position, in well-drained, alkaline soil. H 60cm (2ft)

RECOMMENDED PLANTS:
S. caucasica 'Fama Deep Blue' – large purple-blue flowers. H 60cm (2ft)
S. caucasica 'Fama White' – large white flowers. H 60cm (2ft)
S. columbaria subsp. *ochroleuca* – a scaled-down version of giant scabious, *Cephalaria gigantea*, with the same cool yellow-green flowers but much smaller and produced on wiry stems where they jostle and float from late summer to mid-autumn. H 90cm (3ft)

SPACING: 30cm (1ft) apart.

WHEN TO HARVEST: Late summer, look for tight pincushion centres with the outer petals open.

CONDITIONING AND VASE LIFE: 7–10 days.

USES: As a focal in meadow-style arrangements with other first-year-flowering perennials such as *Achillea* (yarrow), *Silene vulgaris* (bladder campion) and *Catanache caerulea* (cupid's dart) which all work very well together. It is also a classic supporting flower with roses. *S. columbaria* subsp. *ochroleuca* is a good textural accent flower – use tall stems that will dance above the other flowers. Their unusual moonlit colour acts as pinpoints of light, in a similar way to meadow buttercups in late spring.

PROPAGATION: By seed sown in the autumn or spring. Sow every year to ensure continuity of flower.

Top: *Scabiosa caucasica* 'Fama White'
Above: *Scabiosa caucasica* 'Perfecta Blue'

Selinum wallichianum
Milk parsley

I value the addition of umbels in an arrangement to take it beyond the garden and make it convey something of wild, unkempt places. Over the years I have grown many annual forms, but sadly it has become increasingly difficult to produce healthy plants because of the spread of viruses by aphids. Interestingly, perennial umbellifers seem unaffected, so I am on a quest to discover as many harvestable ones as possible. I discovered this one on a visit to Beth Chatto's garden. The mounds of fern-like foliage send up smart purple-suffused stems which are topped by billowing clouds of white umbels in late summer through to early autumn. It likes partial shade in moist soil. H 1.5m (5ft)

SPACING: 45cm (17½in) apart.

WHEN TO HARVEST: When the stems feel ripe and the flowers are open but not fluffy.

CONDITIONING AND VASE LIFE: Sear for 20 seconds; 7–10 days.

USES: Both the flowers and lacy foliage bring a gentle naturalism to arrangements.

PROPAGATION: It resents disturbance, so by seed in early spring, it will flower in its second year.

Selinum wallichianum, the last umbellifer to flower in our fields, taking this shape through to mid-autumn. The burgundy stems pick out the shades of richly coloured dahlias and fruiting woody cuts.

Silene vulgaris
Bladder campion

This native wild flower is a hard-working staple on our farm – it is incredibly productive and easy to grow, producing two generous crops in a season. The delicate grey-green stems are topped with pale green balloon-like calyces. As the calyces mature they are ringed with a fringe of snow-white petals. H 45cm (17½in)

RECOMMENDED PLANTS:
A strain called 'Blushing Lanterns' has more blushed pink on the calyces. H 50cm (19½in)

SPACING: 30cm (1ft) apart

CULTIVATION TIPS: Cut back after the first flush of flowers to encourage a generous second crop.

WHEN TO HARVEST: Early summer, can be cut when in pod or full flower.

CONDITIONING AND VASE LIFE: 7–10 days.

USES: A textural supporting flower which naturalizes arrangements with its wild-flower credentials. The neutral colour means it's a great mixer.

PROPAGATION: Easy from seed sown in early spring, it will flower profusely from early summer in its first year.

Silene vulgaris 'Blushing Lanterns', this dusky bladder campion was introduced to me by Erin Benzakein of the famed Floret flower farm. It has all the credentials to make it the perfect supporting flower – neutral colouring, highly productive and easy from seed.

Solidago rugosa 'Fireworks'

Solidago rugosa '**Fireworks**'
Goldenrod

I had never been enthusiastic about goldenrod until I found this cultivar at a rare plant fair. It has a much finer form than its denser relatives and is less invasive. In late summer it produces arching branched sprays of tiny golden daisy flowers. H 1m (3¼ft)

SPACING: 30cm (1ft) apart

WHEN TO HARVEST: When the flowers on the primary stem in the spray are open.

CONDITIONING AND VASE LIFE: 10 days.

USES: The cascading branches of this elegant form look wonderful in a late-summer arrangement with other golden shades including sunflowers, rudbeckia and guelder rose berries.

PROPAGATION: By basal shoots in spring or division after 3-4 years.

Stachys byzantina
Lamb's ear

A tactile foliage plant with felted minty-silver leaves which I grow to expand the range of supporting foliage colours on offer in late spring, which are mostly fresh, bright greens. It is at its best in bud just before its woolly spires begin to flower. It quickly produces a spreading mat of foliage with plenty of stems for cutting. Full sun and well-drained soil. H 40cm (15½in)

SPACING: 30cm (1ft) apart

WHEN TO HARVEST: When the flowering stems feel firm but have not yet flowered.

CONDITIONING AND VASE LIFE: Sear for 10 seconds; 7–10 days.

USES: A good supporting foliage in bouquet work, where it can nestle in among the flowers.

PROPAGATION: By division in spring, every 3 years to ensure quality and productivity.

Stachys byzantina at the perfect stage for cutting.

Succisella inflexa 'Frosted Pearls'
Devil's Bit Scabious

Tall, spreading branches carry swarms of pink buds which open to small rounded scabious-like flowers in the palest pearly lavender from late summer to early autumn. Like scabious, it is an excellent nectar source for bees. As a damp meadow plant, it enjoys moist soil and will even be happy in heavy clay, unlike the rest of the scabious family. The green, textural seedheads that follow prolong the harvesting period.
H 80cm (2¾ft)

RECOMMENDED PLANTS:
Succisa pratensis (devil's bit scabious) is very similar but has lavender-blue flowers.
H 80cm (2¾ft)

SPACING: 30cm (1ft) apart.

WHEN TO HARVEST: Once the primary flower on the stem is open.

CONDITIONING AND VASE LIFE: 7–10 days.

USES: As an airy accent, since the small pearly flowers on fine branching stems create a transparent, hazy effect.

PROPAGATION: By division in spring.

Succisella inflexa 'Frosted Pearls' is a graceful accent plant and highly prized by pollinators. The branched airy structure of its stems and pearly flower heads lift the saturated colours and density of dahlias.

Symphyotrichum ericoides 'Rosy Veil'
Aster

I was almost ready to give up on asters as a cut flower as they felt a little frumpy, when I chanced upon this treasure at the Great Dixter plant fair. To find one in a creamy-pink, a colour far more compatible with the season, felt like my lucky day. The small daisies are produced en masse in a foaming fountain of arching sprays in early autumn. It is drought-tolerant and mildew-resistant. Asters prefer humus-rich soil that does not dry out too much. H 1m (3¼ft)

RECOMMENDED PLANTS:
S. cordifolium 'Elegans' – plumes of tiny flowers in palest violet in mid-autumn. H 1.2m (4ft)
S. 'Prairie Purple' – tall, early-flowering, stems and foliage flushed dark purple, starry lilac-purple flowers. H 1.3m (4¼ft)

S. turbinellum – the prairie aster, flowering from mid-autumn, with lavender-blue finely rayed flowers that are well spaced on stems with narrow leaves, creating a lightweight, airy appearance. H 1m (3¼ft)

SPACING: 45cm (17½in) apart.

CULTIVATION TIPS: Chelsea chop taller varieties to prevent them flopping and to stagger flowering time.

WHEN TO HARVEST: When a third of the flowers are open on the stem.

CONDITIONING AND VASE LIFE: 7 days.

USES: The arching, frothy stems are the perfect supporter to lighten heavier focal flowers like dahlias.

PROPAGATION: Although these are mildew resistant cultivars they will suffer if overcrowded, so divide in spring every three to five years.

Below left: *Symphyotrichum ericoides* 'Rosy Veil'

Right from top: *Symphyotrichum turbinellum*, *S. cordifolium* 'Elegans', *S.* 'Prairie Purple'

Tellima grandiflora
Fringe cups

A graceful woodland plant that loves a shady spot and seems to cope with relatively dry conditions, this has slender stems studded with fringed cup-like flowers in late spring. The rosettes of vine-shaped leaves clump up and spread, allowing plenty of potential for more plants. H 60cm (2ft)

RECOMMENDED PLANTS:
T. grandiflora Rubra Group – pink-fringed cups. H 60cm (2ft)

SPACING: 30cm (1ft) apart.

WHEN TO HARVEST: When two-thirds of the cups are open and the stems feel firm.

CONDITIONING AND VASE LIFE: Sear for 10 seconds; 7 days.

USES: Once cut, the stems take on curvy shapes as they bend and twist, providing a perfect accent element.

PROPAGATION: Division in early spring.

Tellima grandiflora Rubra Group's slender green spires are studded with fragrant creamy cups.

Thalictrum
Meadow rue

This is an ethereal beauty with ferny foliage and slender stems, topped with clouds of tiny individual lilac or white flowers. By selecting a few species it is possible to spread their flowering season from early to late summer. Their delicate appearance is misleading as they are in fact tough, easy-to-grow plants which thrive in partial shade with humus-rich soil. The large inflorescences do 'frothy' with so much more style than the ubiquitous florists' gypsophila.

RECOMMENDED PLANTS:
T. 'Elin' – a towering giant, which I grow mainly for its striking foliage, which is blue-green flushed with bronze. Picked in mid-spring, it is a great foil for tulips and hellebores. The smoky clouds of flowers in midsummer are reminiscent of smokebush, creating a misty haze in large arrangements. H 2.4m (8ft)

Thalictrum delavayi 'Album', at the right stage for picking with its florets in bud.

T. SPLENDIDE WHITE – tapered panicles of pure white flowers mid to late summer and fresh lime-green ferny foliage which cuts well in early summer. H 1.5m (5ft)

SPACING: 45cm apart.

CULTIVATION TIPS: If the soil is rich, stake to avoid kinky stems.

WHEN TO HARVEST: The finely dissected foliage resembling a maidenhair fern cuts well from late spring. For flowers, cut when the individual florets are still in bud.

CONDITIONING AND VASE LIFE: 7 days.

USES: A lacy supporter for summer focal flowers.

PROPAGATION: Species forms can be raised from freshly collected seed. Cultivars by division once they have formed a good clump.

Valeriana officinalis
Valerian

This tall and upright plant has airy branching stems bearing fragrant clouds of lightly domed blush-pink umbels in early summer, followed by biscuit-coloured frothy seedheads. The flowers are a magnet for pollinators and the cut stems lend an informal, naturalistic feel to arrangements. For sturdy stems, give it a rich, moist soil in full sun. H 1.2m (4ft)

RECOMMENDED PLANTS:
V. pyrenaica – scented, pale pink umbels are flower in late spring. H 1.2m (4ft)

SPACING: 30cm (1ft) apart.

WHEN TO HARVEST: The flowers should only just be opening, otherwise they will drop quickly.

CONDITIONING AND VASE LIFE: 5 days.

USES: I often combine the umbel flowers with the spire shapes of foxgloves and the soft yellow-green of giant scabious.

PROPAGATION: Self seeds freely or collect the seed and sow whilst fresh.

Valeriana officinalis, clouds of vanilla-scented umbels.

Verbascum 'Southern Charm'
Mullein

Like all mulleins, this is classed as a short-lived perennial but I find this hybrid comes back reliably year after year, flowering abundantly in early summer. The colours are mouth-wateringly good – muted, brownish-apricots, pinks and lilacs, each with a deep wine-red eye. It is happy in full sun and well-drained soil. H 90cm (3ft)

SPACING: 30cm (1ft) apart.

CULTIVATION TIPS: Cut back after flowering to encourage a second flush in late summer.

WHEN TO HARVEST: Once half the florets are open.

CONDITIONING AND VASE LIFE: Sear; 5 days.

USES: The spire-shaped flowers create pleasingly kinky shapes which mirror foxgloves in both colour and form. Their dark eyes can be picked up by pairing them with *Sanguisorba menziesii*.

PROPAGATION: By seed in early spring.

Verbascum 'Southern Charm' has a unique colour range for early summer.

Veronicastrum virginicum
Culver's root

Veronica-like tapers in candelabra clusters are borne on tall, robust stems clothed in whorls of leaves. They take the spire-shaped baton from the early summer- flowering delphiniums and foxgloves. Despite their lofty stature, they do not require staking. They are self-sufficient, easy-to-grow perennials which are quicker to bulk up than veronicas, so they make a good substitute. They are also a mecca for bees and butterflies. Position in full sun and moisture-retentive soil.

RECOMMENDED PLANTS:
V. virginicum 'Album' – slender spires in a pale, pinkish white. H 1.6m (5¼ft)
V. virginicum 'Lavendelturm' – glowing pinkish-lilac spikes. H 1.5m (5ft)

SPACING: 45cm (17½in) apart in double rows.

WHEN TO HARVEST: Once the close-set flowers on the primary spire are half open. Stems can be picked for their foliage before flowering; I particularly like the bronzed foliage of 'Album' and the candelabra-shaped flowers make one of the most interesting deep chestnut coloured seedheads.

CONDITIONING AND VASE LIFE: 7 days.

USES: Maximize length and use as a vertical accent in tall arrangements.

PROPAGATION: By division in spring or autumn.

Veronicastrum virginicum 'Fascination', at 1.7m (5½ft), is the tallest cultivar. It has rosy-lilac flower spikes which are prone to fasciation.

Climbers

Generically known as 'vines' in the floral world, climbers are much sought-after for unconstrained, wild displays. Including just a few of their curving stems implies motion, inviting the eye to move around the arrangement; they stretch beyond the main body of it, creating negative space and a feeling of light and air. Whether they are flowering or foliage trails, the movement and space they impart makes all the climbers wonderful accent elements. However, I grow only a few for cutting as they are difficult to support and harvest efficiently.

Climbers have a long harvest window, starting in late spring with honeysuckle and going through to the autumn with the silky seedheads of clematis. Although the range you can grow for cutting is relatively limited, many have more than one stage of harvest; for example, we go on picking jasmine for its foliage long after it has flowered and everlasting sweet pea for its rattling pods as it dries and turns wheaten shades.

The climbers listed here share similar qualities: they are all vigorous growers, needing little attention, and don't mind being cut back hard in late winter. This keeps them contained and provides fresh growth to harvest from midsummer onwards. I use all kinds of structures to support them, from cylinders of galvanized netting to reinforced steel mesh. All of our walls, arches and fencing are seen as a climbing opportunity.

Once established in a sunny, sheltered position, climbers will get bigger and better year on year with just an annual prune and a generous mulch. Apart from securing the framework of climbing plants with tying in, I try not to constrain them any further as it impedes harvesting their generous long trails.

Below: Our central path is flanked by climbers growing on panels of reinforced steel mesh.

Clematis
Clematis

I try to rein in my love for clematis as I know they are a fiddle to support and pick efficiently; it is just that their wiry stems are so good at twining and roaming through an arrangement, adeptly mimicking their natural growth habit. For vase life and productivity I favour the smaller-flowered group three clematis, which flower from midsummer through to autumn. They are rampant growers, demanding space and tall, sturdy supports; I use large-mesh steel reinforcement panels that they can scramble up and cascade over, producing the trailing stems that are the easiest to harvest. They like warm shoots and cool roots, so partial shade is ideal and deep, fertile soil.

RECOMMENDED PLANTS:
C. 'Kaiu' – I spotted this exquisite variety dominating a towering obelisk at RHS Wisley. For a good three months it is smothered in dainty, pink-tinged, bell-shaped flowers. These are produced

Top: *Clematis* 'Kaiu'
Bottom left: *Clematis tangutica*
Bottom right: *Clematis* 'Paul Farges'

on strong, wiry stems that hold the flowers at a pleasing nodding angle in arrangements.

C. 'Paul Farges' – a vigorous climber that produces an abundance of creamy clusters of fragrant flowers with prominent stamens. It is rather like a cultivated version of the wild *Clematis vitalba*.

C. tangutica – nodding, yellow lantern-like flowers, followed by glistening silky seedheads in autumn.

SPACING: 2m (6½ft) apart.

WHEN TO HARVEST: When a quarter of the flowers are open on a stem.

CONDITIONING AND VASE LIFE: Cut the stems long enough to retain some of the woody section as this helps them to take up water; 7 days.

USES: An accent flower to trail and weave through other flowers.

PROPAGATION: Buy 2-year-old plants from a specialist clematis nursery.

Jasminum officinale
Common jasmine

I grow this sweetly scented climber primarily for its fine pinnate foliage – the heady fragrance of the transient flowers is a fleeting bonus, but it is after they have faded that I really start to harvest the long, twining stems. They are one of the best materials for creating a wild outline. Once established, the plants grow vigorously and retain their leaves into autumn, displaying good colour. They need a sunny, sheltered position, ideally on a south-facing wall, to thrive and be abundant. H 2.5m (8¼ft)

RECOMMENDED PLANTS:
J. o. 'Clotted Cream' – larger, cream-coloured flowers with a stronger fragrance.

SPACING: 1.5m (5ft) apart.

The small fragrant white flowers of *Jasminum officinale* are not the main reason we grow a long row of it on the farm. It is for the twining stems which add so much dynamism to arrangements.

WHEN TO HARVEST: For foliage, after flowering when the stems feel ripe late summer to mid autumn.

CONDITIONING AND VASE LIFE: Sear if still in flower; 7–10 days.

USES: I often add jasmine at the final stage of making an arrangement – a few stems can be transformative, adding plenty of air and movement.

PROPAGATION: By layering or hardwood cuttings.

Lathyrus latifolius
Broad-leaved everlasting pea

This vigorous herbaceous climber is more than capable of reaching 2m (6½ft) in a season. What it lacks in scent it more than makes up for in the sheer volume of long, trailing stems it supplies from midsummer all the way through to early autumn. It is reliable and easy to grow. For the best flowers it needs plenty of sunshine.

RECOMMENDED PLANTS: *L. latifolius* 'Rosa Perle' – pale green buds open to sprays of pink pea flowers ranging in shade from rosy to blush.

Lathyrus latifolius 'Rosa Perle'

SPACING: 1m (3¼ft) apart.

WHEN TO HARVEST: When half the flowers on a raceme are open. It can also be picked when it has developed seed pods.

CONDITIONING AND VASE LIFE: 10 days.

USES: The wiry winged stems and clinging tendrils are wonderful for weaving and trailing through other stems in the vase, reflecting its natural growth habit.

PROPAGATION: From seed sown in autumn or early spring.

Lonicera × americana
American woodbine

A classic cottage-garden plant, honeysuckle has trailing stems that are great at disrupting any arrangement that is looking too tidy. I found this rather special hybrid at a rare plant fair and was impressed by its vigorous growth and generous amounts of fragrant flowers. It is an early variety, flowering in late spring, when whorls of pink tubular buds open to reveal creamy-yellow throats. It does best in part shade and moist but well-drained soil. H 2.5m (8¼ft)

RECOMMENDED PLANTS: For a succession of flowers, try *L. periclymenum* 'Graham Thomas' for a good, long-flowering yellow and to follow on through to mid-autumn *L. periclymenum* 'Serotina', a strongly scented red and pink variety.

WHEN TO HARVEST: Once half the tubular flowers are open.

CONDITIONING AND VASE LIFE: 7 days.

USES: As an accent element, with the twining stems adding movement and character. The bi-coloured flowers act as a colour bridge, linking pinks, yellows and peaches together.

PROPAGATION: Easy from semi-ripe cuttings in summer.

Lonicera × americana is often in flower by mid- spring; its deep pink buds pair beautifully with apple blossom and spring bulbs.

Grasses

The addition of just a few stems of a grass to an arrangement powerfully evokes a sense of the wilder landscape beyond the garden, the places where summer meadows sway and shimmer in the breeze, their delicate flowers and seedheads illuminated by the setting sun. This ability to capture the wind and the sun translates to the vase, where grasses bring a suggestion of movement and light. As a group they are collectively the best example of an accent plant, the finishing touch that brings the arrangement to life.

Whether an insubstantial haze, a silky tassel or feathery plume, grasses bring soft textures to arrangements. Their diaphanous nature adds volume without being heavy. Many are virtually transparent, creating a screen through which to see other flowers. Their neutral colours provide a background to bold hues.

Most grasses are at their best from midsummer to mid-autumn, making them natural companions for late summer-flowering perennials. They are also perfectly timed to help lighten and contrast with the rather stiff formality of dahlias. Their season of interest is often prolonged beyond their flowering time by elegant seedheads which can hold their form well into winter; I often harvest miscanthus plumes for Christmas. Others display rich autumn colour, particularly the panicums, which I use just for their foliage after the flowers have finished. Grasses also last an incredibly long time in the vase – many will dry slowly and preserve their form far better this way than when they are hung upside-down.

The grasses listed here are all hardy perennials which are easy to grow on well-drained soil. Many are drought tolerant and are not troubled by pests or disease. Apart from *Stipa gigantea* (giant oat grass), they are deciduous and need little attention apart from a haircut in late winter. All grasses are clump-forming and it is straightforward to propagate established clumps by division when they are in active growth in late spring

However, my most productive grasses are all species produced from seed. They

Harvesting from hedge of *Miscanthus sinensis* hybrids, grown from seed just four years earlier.

take a couple of years to become a free-flowering plant, but it is a cost-effective way to go about growing grasses if you need large quantities.

Bouteloua gracilis 'Blonde Ambition'
Blue grama grass

I first spotted this uniquely shaped grass in the display beds at Arvensis Perennials in Wiltshire. On first impressions it looked like hundreds of blonde eyebrows wafting about in the breeze. The inflorescences, suspended horizontally on fine stems, start out as chartreuse before ageing to a blonde seedhead. They like full sun and dry, well-drained soil. H 1m (3¼ft)

SPACING: 50cm (19½in) apart.

WHEN TO HARVEST: It can be picked at any stage from midsummer to mid-autumn.

CONDITIONING AND VASE LIFE: 14 days, or leave it in the vase to dry.

USES: The invisible stems allow the 'eyebrows' to hover among other flowers in a truly gestural way. It pairs well with other North American prairie perennials such as aster and echinacea.

PROPAGATION: Divide every 3-5 years in early to mid-spring.

Bouteloua gracilis 'Blonde Ambition'

Briza media
Doddering dillies

The miniature perennial form of quaking grass, in late spring the tight mounds of semi-evergreen foliage produce wiry stems bedecked with delicate panicles of purple-tinged, heart-shaped flowers. These clouds of little lockets bob and shiver in the slightest breeze. Full sun and a moist soil for good stem length. H 60cm (2ft)

SPACING: 30cm (1ft) apart.

WHEN TO HARVEST: The flowers should be closed and tight.

CONDITIONING AND VASE LIFE: 10 days.

USES: It creates a glittering effect in an arrangement as the dangling lockets catch the light. I like pairing it with other delicate flowers such as Icelandic poppies and buttercups. It dries well, too.

PROPAGATION: Sow in autumn. Established clumps can be divided in spring.

Briza media

Calamagrostis brachytricha
Korean feather reed grass

A clump-forming, upright grass which produces mounds of feathery plumes flushed smoky purple, this is an adaptable, easy-to-grow plant. For the best colour and upright habit, grow it in full sun. It is a slow spreader, taking two to five years to reach its full size. The plumes make a good alternative to spire-shaped flowers in the autumn, when the latter are relatively scarce. A few plants go a long way as it forms generous clumps by its second year. H 1m (3¼ft)

RECOMMENDED PLANTS:
Calamagrostis varia is an earlier-flowering species, more deeply coloured and with a slightly looser form.

SPACING: 50cm (19½in) apart.

WHEN TO HARVEST: In late summer, when they have a good flush of colour. The flowers turn green and then tan as they age.

CONDITIONING AND VASE LIFE: 7–10 days.

USES: Their fluffy, tactile texture is the perfect softener for the rather stiff forms of dahlias. The flowers also dry well – place them with the stems upright, as this will help them to remain open and feathery.

PROPAGATION: By seed in or division in early spring.

Bleached of colour, the feathery seedheads of *Calamagrostis brachytricha* retain their form well into winter.

Chasmanthium latifolium
Spangle grass

This unusual woodland grass has arching stems bearing dangling panicles of flattened oat-like flowers, which turn from olive green to bronze. It is clump-forming, with bamboo-like leaves that colour to gold in the autumn. For good stem length and fresh-looking foliage, grow it in moist soil with some shade. H 60cm (2ft)

SPACING: 45cm (17½in) apart.

WHEN TO HARVEST: I like to use spangle grass when both the leaves and flowers have turned gold and bronze in mid-autumn.

CONDITIONING AND VASE LIFE: Stems dry in the vase, giving weeks of interest.

USES: For impact, use stems in small clusters through an arrangement. To dry, harvest when the stems are still green to prevent shattering. Place in a vase with a small amount of water, do not replenish and they will dry slowly from the bottom up, retaining the shape of the nodding flowers.

PROPAGATION: Sow from seed or divide in early spring.

The flattened bronze seedheads of *Chasmanthium latifolium* reflect the light as they dangle from invisibly fine stems.

Melica altissima 'Alba'
Siberian melic

This unassuming treasure of an early-flowering grass is ready to pick in late spring. It has dainty grain-like white flowers which dance about and sparkle on slender stems. As a woodlander, it enjoys partial shade. It can cope with dry soil, but to increase the rather diminutive stem length a little moisture is beneficial. H 45cm (17½in)

Right: *Melica altissima* 'Alba'

Below: *Melica ciliata*, is later flowering coinciding with other first-year-flowering perennials such as *Achillea ptarmica* 'The Pearl'

RECOMMENDED PLANTS: *M. ciliata* – pale buff spikes in midsummer. H 50cm (19½in)

SPACING: 30cm (1ft) apart.

CONDITIONING AND VASE LIFE: 7 days.

USES: I use the graceful bedecked stems as a highlighter in small arrangements. It pairs well with other dainty perennials such as geums, ranunculus and polemoniums.

PROPAGATION: Divide clumps in early spring.

Miscanthus sinensis
Silver grass

The largest and latest flowering grass I grow, it needs space to develop, which takes about three years. Now at it's full stately size, it makes an effective shelter belt in our exposed field, filtering the wind with a reassuring rustle. Once late-summer flowers are pollinated, they fluff and crimp into smoky plumes. They hold beautifully at this stage, which extends their season into late autumn. It is easy to grow; position it in full sun and soil which does not completely dry out. H 1.5–2m (5– 6½ft)

RECOMMENDED PLANTS: *M. sinensis* 'Malepartus' is early-flowering, producing silky mahogany tassels that fade to a pinkish buff.

SPACING: 1m (3¼ft) apart.

WHEN TO HARVEST: Late summer silky tassels or late autumn smoky plumes.

CONDITIONING AND VASE LIFE: 10 days.

USES: I prefer using the flowers dried, either with fresh chrysanthemums or in a wreath with other dried materials. For a loose, open shape, dry upright.

PROPAGATION: By seed in early spring or division of established clumps in late spring.

Miscanthus sinensis, by mid-autumn the silky tassels begin to fluff up as they go to seed.

Oryzopsis miliacea
Smilo grass

This treasure was introduced to me by Charlotte Reed, one of the G&G team, who also happens to have her own plant nursery. As an avid attendee of rare plant fairs she is always finding new treasures. This was a real find; flowering from early summer all the way through till late autumn, it produces delicate whorls of flowers that glint gold when they catch the sun. It likes full sun and well-drained soil. The stems are fairly fragile, so it is best in a sheltered position. H 1m (3¼ft)

SPACING: 50cm (19½in) apart.

WHEN TO HARVEST: When the whorls are open and green.

CONDITIONING AND VASE LIFE: Infinite, as it dries in the vase.

Oryzopsis miliacea glinting in the afternoon sun.

USES: It suits light, airy arrangements with plenty of room to show off its delicate structure. Make the most of the height and size of the flowers and go for a tall vase with accompanying rangy flowers such as scabious and gaura.

PROPAGATION: It self seeds freely, so I have found transplanting the seedlings is one of the easiest ways to gain more plants.

Panicum virgatum 'Rehbraun'
Switch grass

I grow this subtle deciduous grass for the hazy effect that its maroon spikelets create in early autumn, with the added bonus of deep burgundy leaves later in the season. Its prairie origins give it a wild, relaxed elegance, but I would recommend planting a few as it does need to be used generously to make an impact. Switch grass likes to be grown in full sun and does not enjoy a rich soil; lean and mean will produce the strongest plants and retain its upright habit. H 1.2m (4ft)

RECOMMENDED PLANTS:
P. virgatum 'Squaw', 'Warrior' and 'Shenandoah' are all very similar in habit and colour.

SPACING: 30cm (1ft) apart.

WHEN TO HARVEST: The spikelets should have good rich colour, not turning to tan.

CONDITIONING AND VASE LIFE: 10 days.

USES: A good textural supporting flower to soften dahlias. The autumnal foliage adds flashes of colour and is brilliant at picking out similar tones in chrysanthemums.

PROPAGATION: Divide in late spring when in growth.

Panicum virgatum 'Rehbraun'

Pennisetum villosum
Feathertop

The longest-flowering and most productive grass I grow, it has graceful, arching clumps of fine leaves covered in a halo of soft greeny-white bottlebrush flowers. Despite being warned that it is not hardy, I have found that mine return year after year, even with our cold, wet winters. Position in full sun and add grit to improve the drainage. Cutting lots of stems every week perpetuates the flowering period from midsummer right through to the first frosts. H 60cm (2ft)

RECOMMENDED PLANTS: *P. orientale* and its many cultivars are the hardiest species. I have found the following survive our winters and have good height.
P. orientale 'Karley Rose' – a dusky pink beige. H 90cm (3ft)
P. orientale 'Tall Tails' - pale and wispy flowers. H 1.2m (4ft)

SPACING: 30cm (1ft) apart.

Pennisetum villosum

WHEN TO HARVEST: The flowers should be fully formed, firm and a lustrous, creamy-green. Once they have released their pollen they fade to buff and start to disintegrate.

CONDITIONING AND VASE LIFE: 7 days.

USES: The fluffy flowers create a soft, blurry effect in arrangements, evoking a dreamy, ethereal feeling. Their narrow arching leaves are an added bonus, draping over the side of the vase.

PROPAGATION: Division in late spring or from seed in early spring for first year flowering.

Stipa gigantea
Giant oat grass

One of the earliest and largest grasses for cutting, in midsummer its shimmering, oat-like flowers break open, hovering at head height; their large panicles glisten like old gold in the long evening light. They are beautifully transparent and even after the awns have dispersed their seed they hold their shape well. This stately grass needs plenty of space, full sun and well-drained soil. H 1.8m (6ft)

RECOMMENDED PLANTS: 'Goldilocks' – a compact form that retains its large flowers. H 1.5m (5ft)

SPACING: 1.5m (5ft) apart.

WHEN TO HARVEST: They are at their best in midsummer with their dangling anthers, but their seedheads look good all the way through to early autumn.

CONDITIONING AND VASE LIFE: Like all grasses, they gradually dry in the vase.

USES: Their golden airiness means they can be arranged with all manner of other flowers without taking over. They create a glinting veil-like backdrop with just a few stems.

PROPAGATION: By division in late spring every 3 years.

Stipa gigantea, a transparent flowering panicle in midsummer.

Trees and shrubs

Trees and shrubs are the foundation of our planting on the flower farm; they define the boundaries and shelter the other plants, and us at times. Also known as 'woody cuts', they provide year-round material for the framework and supporting elements in an arrangement, performing a similar role to the one they have in the garden, acting as a structural foil for the flowers.

The majority of the 40 trees and shrubs listed here are deciduous, because they are generally hardier and faster growing. They are all are tried and tested plants which have been put through their paces on our farm. It is a very flat and open site, exposed to the elements, so plants that grow quickly and create shelter while simultaneously providing plenty of cutting material characterize my selection.

It takes at least three to five years before shrubs and certainly trees can be tentatively harvested, so if you have a new garden it is wise to get going and plant them first – possibly as a cutting hedge to create shelter for future flowers. Much of my selection consists of well-known garden plants that are commonly available from nurseries. To keep the costs down, I recommend trying to source bare-root stock to be planted in the dormant season where possible. They tend to establish and grow away more quickly too, especially with a dose of mycorrhizal fungi.

I rely on deciduous woody cut stems to define the seasons, from fresh new leaves and early spring or summer blossom to fruits and autumn colour. Even the characterful shapes of bare branches, perhaps tasselled with catkins, speak clearly of the time of year and make natural companions for what else is in season. There are some that offer more than one stage of harvest, with attractive foliage, flowers and fruits. For these workhorses I grow larger amounts as I know harvesting a shrub for its bronzed leaves is sacrificing the early spring flowers that are promised on that same wood.

For cutting, trees and shrubs can generally be spaced closer together than usual in a garden situation, especially if you are trying to create a cutting hedge-cum-windbreak. Once planted, they are mulched with bark chip and irrigation lines are laid. We make generous paths between the rows to accommodate their future growth. These are covered with landscape fabric to keep them weed- and mud-free. Once established they are mostly very happy to just get on with growing, as long as they are picked, in effect pruned, annually to maintain their shape and vigour.

Although trees and shrubs are quite an investment initially, with time and only a little bit of effort they will provide you with an abundance of characterful and unique 'woody cuts' all year round.

Abelia × grandiflora
Glossy abelia

A relaxed, loose habit makes this semi-evergreen shrub the perfect candidate for natural-style arrangements. Its arching branches are clothed in small, deep green, glossy oval leaves. From midsummer through to late autumn, a steady succession of abundant pink-flushed white tubular flowers are produced. They are honey-scented and much loved by bees. When the flowers are spent the bronze pink calyces remain on the stem and add another colour and texture to the stems. Abelias require a sheltered, sunny position in well-drained soil as they can be tender. H 2.5m (8¼ft)

RECOMMENDED PLANTS: *A. mosanensis* has deliciously fragrant flowers in early summer and is hardier than *A. × grandiflora*. H 1.5m (5ft)

SPACING: 1m apart

CULTIVATION TIPS: Remove older wood in early spring to encourage vigorous new shoots from the base. Renewal prune by cutting everything back hard every 3 years.

WHEN TO HARVEST: Branches can be picked for their flowers or just the remaining calyces.

CONDITIONING AND VASE LIFE: Woody cut; 10–14 days.

USES: I tend to use abelia in autumnal arrangements, paired with claret dahlias and bronzy chrysanthemums.

Abelia × grandiflora

Alnus cordata
Italian alder

I grow alder for the bare branches, which carry a combination of long, dangling mahogany catkins and purplish-brown upright cones. It makes an incredibly tough, fast-growing hedge that copes with both waterlogged soil and exposed hillsides, so if you need to create a windbreak for other plants it is a very good candidate. H 2.5m (8¼ft)

RECOMMENDED PLANTS: *A. glutinosa* is the British native version, with smaller leaves and catkins. I forage this one, as it grows all along the river banks beside our farm. H 3m (10ft) if grown as a hedge.

SPACING: 50cm (19½in) apart.

CULTIVATION TIPS: If growing as a hedge, trim back hard in late summer. This is probably best done every other year to keep the vigorous growth under control.

WHEN TO HARVEST: In late winter.

CONDITIONING AND VASE LIFE: Woody cut. 21 days at the catkin stage.

USES: I pick catkin branches long and use them as stand-alone arrangements or to create a bold framework for forced narcissus. Branches can be used as a framework element when in leaf, in a similar way to beech and hornbeam.

PROPAGATION: Buy bare root hedging plants during dormant season.

Alnus glutinosa, displaying its winter catkins and cones, along the river bank next to the farm.

Amelanchier lamarckii
Juneberry

This small versatile deciduous tree offers year-round interest. In mid-spring the flowerbuds open to fleeting white star-shaped blossoms accompanied by emerging soft coppery foliage. It is in the limelight again as the season ends, with striking crimson autumn colour. It prefers a neutral to slightly acidic soil and plenty of moisture to grow well. H 2.5m (8¼ft).

SPACING: For productivity, grow it as a double, staggered hedge at 45cm (17½in) apart.

WHEN TO HARVEST: Cut branches when the flowers are in bud to prolong vase life.

CONDITIONING AND VASE LIFE: Woody cut; 7 days.

USES: I like to arrange amelanchier when the flowers are still in tight bud – they are like little points of light on dark stems with just a hint of the rosy-bronze foliage that will follow. Their fine branching form adds a stylish, airy framework to heavy-headed tulips and ranunculus and the most pleasing colour combination with soft yellow narcissus.

PROPAGATION: Buy bare root hedging plants during dormant season.

A. lamarckii, one of the earliest blossoming branches, usually flowering in the gap between plum and apple.

Berberis 'Georgei'
Barberry 'Georgei'

This is an overlooked genus for cutting, probably because of the spiny stems. I only discovered this rare beauty because I had been walking past it on my regular dog walk for the past thirteen years. After a chat with the owner I acquired cuttings and it is now happily growing in our field. It is a fountain-shaped, deciduous shrub with pendent racemes of soft yellow flowers in late spring, but its real moment of glory is when these develop into berries. They turn from yellow to deep coral red dangling, glistening beads which weight the stems into pleasing arching shapes. H 2.5m (8¼ft)

SPACING: 1m (3¼ft) apart.

CULTIVATION TIPS: In late winter, thin out some of the older stems to the base to let in air and light.

WHEN TO HARVEST: They can be picked from late summer through to mid-autumn; the berries gradually intensify in colour as the temperature drops.

CONDITIONING AND VASE LIFE: Woody cut; 7 days.

USES: As an autumnal accent that combines with dahlias, zinnias and rudbeckia in a similar colour palette.

Berberis 'Georgei'

PROPAGATION: Hardwood cuttings at leaf fall.

Betula pendula
Silver birch

A deciduous tree with a slender, gently weeping shape, *B. pendula* has delicate, twiggy branches which carry small fluttering leaves. There is a lightness of touch to a birch stem, as it allows for plenty of negative space or, more simply put, 'air'. It is fast-growing and tolerant of all types of soil in full sun. It does not mind an exposed position, so can be grown as part of a shelter belt. Coppicing is the best way to manage birch for cut foliage, as the resulting multiple stems will produce more material per tree and be at a reachable height. H 2.5m (8¼ft)

SPACING: 1.5m (5ft) apart.

Betula pendula turns a buttery yellow in the autumn.

CULTIVATION TIPS: Coppice in late winter, every 3-5 years, when the trunk is no thicker than 5cm.

WHEN TO HARVEST: From early summer through to autumn for foliage branches and after leaf fall for the bare twiggy stems with their small catkins.

CONDITIONING AND VASE LIFE: Woody cut; 7 days.

USES: The drooping, airy branches create a light trailing element in vase arrangements and bouquets. In winter the supple twiggy stems are a good rustic base for wreaths.

PROPAGATION: Buy as bare root saplings in dormant season.

Brachyglottis (Dunedin Group) 'Sunshine'
Senecio

I got to know senecio while designing planting schemes for Oxford's hospitals. It is most commonly used as an amenity shrub, and I always considered it a functional but rather uninspiring plant. Twenty years later my opinion of it changed when I used it as cut foliage, as in this form it is a far more stylish proposition. The ovate leaves are a soft grey-green with a felted texture. It is one of our staples, harvested so frequently it never gets the opportunity to produce its alarmingly neon-yellow, daisy-like flowers. This is a fast-growing, adaptable and drought-tolerant shrub. H 1.2m (4ft)

SPACING: 50cm (19½in) apart.

CULTIVATION TIPS: Responds well to being cut right back in early spring. It will regrow with vigour producing plenty of fresh foliage to harvest from midsummer onwards.

WHEN TO HARVEST: As it is evergreen it can be harvested year round, but is at its best in the summer months.

CONDITIONING AND VASE LIFE: 14 days.

USES: As versatile supporting foliage, it seems to enhance any flower colour. The branching, woody stems make an excellent structural base for bouquets. It is a useful substitute for silvery eucalyptus.

PROPAGATION: Easy from semi-ripe cuttings in midsummer.

The silver foliage of *Brachyglottis* 'Sunshine' has a felted texture which accentuates the softness of its colouring.

Carpinus betulus
Hornbeam

This native tree is most commonly seen as a clipped hedge, but if left untamed it quickly produces slender, elegant arching branches. The foliage is mid-green and has a very pleasing pleated texture. Hornbeams are as tough as they come and will tolerate wet, heavy soil and shade. They are fast-growing and will quickly create shelter and long branches to cut for larger arrangements. H 3m (10ft) with annual tip pruning.

SPACING: For a hedge, plant 45cm (17½in) apart for a single row or 60cm (2ft) for a staggered double row.

Carpinus betulus unfurling its pleated leaves in mid-spring.

CULTIVATION TIPS: Prune out the leading branches to encourage plenty of side growth which will be easier to reach and a more interesting shape to work with.

WHEN TO HARVEST: This has the longest harvest period of all my foliage plants; we start picking budding branches in mid spring and are still picking for golden autumn colour in mid autumn. The leaves stay on the branches through the winter, so it could be used year round if you choose.

CONDITIONING AND VASE LIFE: Woody cut, sear and condition overnight. 7 days.

USES: Hornbeam is my most used framework plant with the longest harvest window.

PROPAGATION: Buy as bare root hedging plants in dormant season.

Choisya × dewitteana
WHITE DAZZLER
Mexican orange blossom

This compact evergreen shrub has slender, dark green, palmate leaves. The foliage is much finer than that of the more ubiquitous *C. ternata* and easier to combine with other flowers. In late spring it is smothered with sweetly scented clusters of white flowers, pink in bud; they resemble orange blossom in both appearance and fragrance. A sunny, sheltered position in well-drained soil is the ideal site for this fast-growing and highly productive shrub which fills a tricky gap in the season. Rich in nectar, the flowers are also greatly appreciated by bees and butterflies. H 1.2m (4ft)

RECOMMENDED PLANTS:
C. × dewitteana APPLE BLOSSOM is a pinker version. H 1.2m (4ft)

CULTIVATION TIPS: If they have not been picked, prune stems immediately after flowering to encourage new wood for next year's flowers.

WHEN TO HARVEST: When the flower buds are just opening.

CONDITIONING AND VASE LIFE: Woody cut; 10–14 days.

USES: The flowering branches are a valuable supporting element in late spring.

PROPAGATION: By semi-ripe cuttings in late summer.

Choisya × dewitteana WHITE DAZZLER

Cornus mas
Cornelian cherry

This rather overlooked large shrub from the dogwood family is a much more refined way of using golden yellow than forsythia in early spring. The dainty, star-shaped flowers, which are a magnet for early pollinators, spangle on naked stems and if picked in bud last incredibly well in water. It is a slow grower, so with picking it will retain a shrub rather than tree size. Position in full sun for the best flower production. H 2.5m (8¼ft)

SPACING: 1.5m (5ft) apart

CULTIVATION TIPS: Flowers are produced on last year's wood which naturally branches from the base, so harvest stems to this framework to encourage next year's crop.

WHEN TO HARVEST: It is best picked in bud and forced indoors.

CONDITIONING AND VASE LIFE: Woody cut; 14 days.

USES: Combine with other early flowering branches, such as pussy willow and cherry plum.

PROPAGATION: Get a head start by planting a containerized plant.

The golden starry flowers of *Cornus mas* – one of the first woody cuts in early spring.

Corylus avellana
Hazel

This British native is brilliant for bringing the countryside into gardens and homes. Despite the fact this is not the slow-growing cultivar 'Contorta', its branches often look crooked and time-weathered. The characterful stems are relatively fast-growing if they are treated as a coppiced hedging plant. Hazels are tough stalwarts, able to withstand freezing temperatures down to -20°C (-4°F), so use them to create shelter and shade for their lower-growing woodland companions. H 3m (10ft) if coppiced every 3 years.

RECOMMENDED PLANTS:
C. maxima 'Purpurea' has dark purple leaves and red catkins which fade to green in the summer. H 3m (10ft)

SPACING: 1.2m (4ft) for coppiced hazel planted in a row for a hedge or screen or in groups of three or five for a woodland bed.

Corylus avellana, good in winter and also invaluable for its young, spring foliage.

CULTIVATION TIPS: In mid-spring, prune and harvest at the same time. Select stems that are more than 2 years old, taking them back to the base about 5cm above the ground. This will encourage vigorous regrowth and reachable catkin-laden stems for the following winter.

WHEN TO HARVEST: In late winter for the showy yellow male catkins. The broadly heart-shaped leaves follow in mid-spring.

CONDITIONING AND VASE LIFE: Woody cut; 7–14 days.

USES: Over the winter months I use the catkins for wreath-making or paired with forced bulbs such as *Narcissus* 'Paper-white'. The small, newly emerged foliage on its kinky stems make it one of my favourite framework plants for spring-flowering bulbs.

PROPAGATION: Buy as bare root hedging plants in the dormant season.

Cotinus coggygria
Smokebush

I grow smokebush primarily for its fluffy flower plumes; in midsummer, this plant looks as if it is wreathed in smoke. The flowers are produced after two years, so these large, fast-growing deciduous shrubs will demand plenty of space if they are to be used for flower production. They do best in full sun and well-drained soil which is not too fertile. A number of cultivars are available, though I favour the natural appearance of the species form, which has small rounded leaves of a soft bluish-green and buff-coloured flowers. H 3m (10ft)

RECOMMENDED PLANTS:
C. 'Grace' is the largest cultivar, with correspondingly large copper-purple leaves and flower panicles measuring 30cm long. We grow it for these impressive purplish-pink clouds. H 3m (10ft) if coppiced every 4-5 years.
C. 'Flame' has large green leaves with the best autumn colour and beautifully coloured dusky pink flowers. H 3m (10ft) if coppiced every 4-5 years.
C. GOLDEN SPIRIT has small acid green leaves which mellow to gold. A good one for foliage. H 2.5m (8¼ft)

SPACING: 1.5m (5ft) with coppicing.

CULTIVATION TIPS: For flowers, coppice every 4-5 years in early spring. Ideally, grow more than one plant so the pruning regime can be alternated. For richly coloured foliage and large leaves, pollard annually.

WHEN TO HARVEST: The flowers mature in early summer and are best picked by late summer. For foliage, wait until late summer when it begins to feel shield-like.

CONDITIONING AND VASE LIFE:
Woody cut and sear for 30 seconds. 7-14 days.

USES: The flowering branches are the perfect large stand-alone arrangement. The flowers dry well and make excellent textural clouds in hanging installations.

PROPAGATION: Softwood cuttings in early summer.

Cotinus 'Grace' produces clouds of copper-purple flowers.

Crataegus monogyna
Common hawthorn

Our farm is surrounded by this native plant in the form of a tall, unruly hedge which never gets cut, just browsed by me and the birds. It is a towering plant that encloses the garden, helping to raise the temperature in summer and soften the blows of the harshest winter weather. Hawthorn is ultra-hardy and adaptable, growing at pace in anything but a bog. It supports hundreds of insect species and is a popular feeding station for our bat population. The bright green leaves are one of the first to emerge in early spring and the red fruits known as haws persist until the migrating fieldfares arrive in late autumn to feast on them.
H 4m (13ft)

RECOMMENDED PLANTS: Some of the larger fruiting species have haws that look similar to crab apples, such as *C. persimilis* 'Prunifolia' and *C. ellwangeriana*. These are better grown as specimen trees.

SPACING: 50cm (19½in) apart.

WHEN TO HARVEST: The thorny branches are quickly clad in lichen and create interesting shapes in winter displays. The bright green, lobed leaves are some of the first to emerge in early spring and hold surprisingly well at this immature stage. The blossom can be used in late spring, but it is short-lived and has a strong, unpleasant smell. The haws, initially bronze then deep red, can be used at any stage of maturity.

CONDITIONING AND VASE LIFE: Woody cut; 7 days.

USES: A framework plant for spring and autumn.

PROPAGATION: Buy as bare root hedging in the dormant season.

Left: *Crataegus persimilis* 'Prunifolia'
Below: *Crataegus monogyna*

Eucalyptus
Eucalyptus

Despite this being the most abundant foliage plant that we grow, it is so popular that the demand for it easily outstrips supply. Its pruning regime means it is only available from autumn through to early spring. This is when it is pollarded to maintain the juvenile stage of its foliage, which has the best colour and fragrance. It also prevents it from turning into a monster-sized tree, which could easily happen with a 1–2m (3¼– 6½ft) rate of growth a year. It is a diverse genus with species to suit a wide range of growing conditions and purposes.

RECOMMENDED PLANTS: The selection I grow cope well with our cold, exposed site and wet winters. They can tolerate -15°C (5°F) and offer a range of leaf shapes and shades of blue-green-grey.

E. archeri is similar to *E. gunnii* but has the addition of flower buds on the second year's growth. Instead of pollarding in the spring we maintain it as pruned bushes so that we can harvest from them through the summer months, giving us a supply of eucalyptus when the other species are regrowing. H 1.5m (5ft)

E. gunnii is very hardy, highly productive and responds vigorously to pollarding. If I could grow only one eucalyptus it would be this well-known all-rounder.

It is good on exposed sites and could be used as a windbreak. The foliage is a glaucous silvery-green, starting off round and elongating as it ages. H 2-3m (6½–10ft) with annual pollarding.

E. nicholii goes by the common name of willow peppermint due to its fine feathery leaves strongly aromatic of eucalyptus and mint and weeping habit, good for wedding work. H 2-3m (6½–10ft) with annual pollarding.

E. parvula, the small-leaved gum, has a bushy habit, attractive maroon stems and small blue-green leaves. H 2-3m (6½–10ft) with annual pollarding.

SPACING: 1.5–2m (5– 6½ft) apart in a row and between rows. The plants need

plenty of space to encourage side growth and a subsequently higher yield.

CULTIVATION TIPS: Plant trees during the growing season using mycorrhizal fungi and water well in the first year. Cut back to a waist-high framework in early spring. To help the regrowth, feed with a slow-release fertilizer in mid-spring and a high potassium one in late summer.

WHEN TO HARVEST: Between mid autumn and mid spring when the new growth has ripened.

CONDITIONING AND VASE LIFE: 10–30 days.

USES: A staple supporting foliage.

PROPAGATION: To save on 1-2 years of growing time, source plants in 3-litre (1-gal) air-rooted pots which stimulate a healthy radial root system. Plants raised from genetically hardy seed will produce tougher plants which can withstand cold winters.

Left to right: *Eucalyptus archeri, E. nicholii, E. gunnii*

Euonymus europaeus
Spindle

A large deciduous shrub famed for its blazing autumn colour and vibrant pink capsules which open to reveal orange fruits in mid autumn. This British hedgerow plant is good in a cutting hedge. Hardy and fast-growing, it makes an excellent shelter belt. The best colour is achieved in full sun. H 3m (10ft).

RECOMMENDED PLANTS: *E. europaeus* 'Red Cascade' produces far more fruits than the species form and also has a deeper intensity of colour. H 3m (10ft)

SPACING: 1.5m (5ft) for a specimen plant or 45cm (17½in) for a double staggered hedge.

Euonymus europaeus 'Red Cascade'

CULTIVATION TIPS: Tip prune young plants in mid to late spring to promote bushy side growth.

WHEN TO HARVEST: When capsules are coloured but before they open.

CONDITIONING AND VASE LIFE: 10 days.

USES: A colourful addition to an autumnal, hedgerow-style arrangement, it combines well with other fruiting branches such as crab apples, haws and rose hips. The framework branches offer support and the colourful capsules make a good bridge between dahlia varieties.

PROPAGATION: Buy as bare-root hedging plants in the dormant season.

Fagus sylvatica
Beech

For cut-foliage purposes, this majestic British native is best grown as a hedge. It will produce a bountiful supply of woody cuts from midsummer all the way through until late autumn. Beech is relatively fast-growing and tolerant of most conditions, apart from waterlogged soil; if you are looking for quicker growth and have wet soil, hornbeam (*Carpinus*) with its similar leaves would be a better choice. I start to harvest branches in late summer when the hornbeam is beginning to look dull and tatty. The beech leaves are still a shiny deep green, but as the seasons change they turn a buttery gold and then fade and crisp to tan.
H 2m (6½ft)

Fagus sylvatica holds well out of water, slowly drying but not dropping its leaves.

RECOMMENDED PLANTS: *F. sylvatica* f. 'Purpurea' – copper beech can also be grown as a hedge. Position in full sun for the best colour and use earlier in the season when it is at its most copper. H 3m (10ft) with tip pruning.

SPACING: For a hedge plant, 45cm (17½in) apart for a single row or 60cm (2ft) for a staggered double row.

CULTIVATION TIPS: Prune or harvest out the leading branches to encourage plenty of side growth which will be easier to reach and more interesting.

WHEN TO HARVEST: Wait until the leaves feel leathery to the touch.

CONDITIONING AND VASE LIFE: Woody cut, sear and condition overnight. 7 days when young and up to 21 days when the leaves have their autumn colour.

USES: Beech responds well to fairly brutal harvesting, regrowing quickly, so it is a useful woody cut for large-scale arrangements and installation work.

PROPAGATION: Source as bare root hedging plants in the dormant season.

Forsythia × *intermedia*
Forsythia

A late winter-flowering shrub, this has vibrant yellow flowers that are enough to wake anyone from their seasonal slumber. It is one of the easiest species to force, with no special treatment needed – just bring the budded branches indoors. The signature flowers are not the only season of interest, since forsythia also has beautifully coloured autumn foliage.
H 2.5m (8¼ft)

RECOMMENDED PLANTS:
F. × *intermedia* 'Lynwood Variety' is the most common cultivar and a prolific producer. It has an upright habit with a good covering of flowers along the stems. H 2.5m (8¼ft)

SPACING: 1.2m (4ft) apart.

WHEN TO HARVEST: I prune out the older branches covered in tight buds and bring them into the house, where the flowers make a brilliant show before the leaves.

CONDITIONING AND VASE LIFE:
14 days from bud.

USES: The tall stems are effective arranged simply on their own.

PROPAGATION: By softwood cuttings in early summer.

A forsythia branch brought indoors in tight bud is flowering a week later. It is by far the easiest woody cut to force requiring nothing more than a warm, bright room.

Hydrangea paniculata
Panicle hydrangea

This is my hydrangea of choice, since the lacy, conical flowers are a much easier shape to work with than the rather incongruous mopheads. Fortunately, *H. paniculata* is the most sun-tolerant species of hydrangea, which suits my open site, but I find they still need to be sheltered and kept well watered for good stem length and flower production. H 1.5 (5ft)

RECOMMENDED PLANTS:
H. paniculata 'Kyushu' – the most delicate and lacy cultivar we grow, also the best for drying. H 1.2m (4ft)
H. paniculata 'Limelight' – commonly grown by cut-flower growers, it has large pyramidal flowerheads in a greenish white. This is my most vigorous and productive cultivar, but even with light pruning the heads can be too large to work with. H 1.5m (5ft)

SPACING: 80cm (2¾ft) apart.

CULTIVATION TIPS: The creamy-white flowers are produced on new wood, so prune in early spring before the new growth starts. For long, straight stems with large panicles, cut back hard to about 15cm. If you prefer branching stems topped with smaller flowers, as I do, prune more lightly to a permanent woody framework.

WHEN TO HARVEST: The flowers can be picked at multiple stages, from immature green in midsummer, peak creaminess in late summer, pink in early autumn and finally dry on the plant in papery shades of buff and tan.

CONDITIONING AND VASE LIFE: Remove most of the foliage. If the flowers are mature they can last 14 days. To dry, hang upside down in a warm, dry room out of direct sunlight.

USES: The woody stems are a useful framework material while the voluminous, creamy panicles are versatile supporting flowers.

PROPAGATION: By softwood cuttings in early summer.

Left to right: The creamy-white flower panicles of *Hydrangea paniculata* 'Pink Diamond' fade to deep pink; *H. paniculata* 'Limelight'; The brown papery flowerheads of *H. paniculata* cultivars stand well into winter.

Hypericum × inodorum
Magical Series
Hypericum

This shrub has been improved for the cut flower trade by the Dutch nursery Kolster. The Magical Series are healthy, robust plants with good rust resistance. They come in a 'kid in a sweet shop' range of glossy, coloured berries and are generally semi-evergreen, with strong, upright bushy growth. I recommend looking at the later-fruiting varieties as berries seem a bit out of place in the summer months. They are easy to grow and highly productive, with some of the earlier varieties producing a second flush in the autumn. To guarantee they do not succumb to rust, give them a humus-rich, moist soil in full sun.

RECOMMENDED PLANTS:
'Magical Beauty' – our earliest and most productive variety with soft peach berries in midsummer and again in early autumn. H 80cm (2¾ft)

'Magical Pumpkin' – chunky coral berries in late summer. H 60cm (2ft)
'Magical Universe' – a handsome cultivar with dark mahogany berries late summer and purplish-green foliage. H 60cm (2ft)

SPACING: 60cm (2ft) apart.

CULTIVATION TIPS: To encourage strong, supporting growth, cut back hard to 5cm in late winter.

WHEN TO HARVEST: The berries should be brightly coloured and shiny. As they age they turn dull and eventually black.

CONDITIONING AND VASE LIFE: Woody cut; 7–14 days.

USES: The woody branching stems support softer flowers and the mid-green foliage is a good foil for other flowers.

PROPAGATION: Semi-hardwood cuttings in late summer.

Hypericum × inodorum 'Magical Pumpkin', the shiny coral berries are an eye-popping supporting element to dahlias.

Lavandula
Lavender

Lavender always reminds me of my grandmother's garden, where harvesting and drying the flowers was an annual ritual. Varieties with rich colour and larger flowers are also lovely used fresh from early to mid summer. I grow cultivars from the two main species: *angustifolia*, which tends to flower earlier, is shorter and sweeter, while *intermedia* is later and taller with larger flowers and a more camphoraceous scent. We grow ours on an area of thin soil overlaying chalk and in full sun.

RECOMMENDED PLANTS:
L. angustifolia ELIZABETH – fragrant large flowers, a good fresh flower. H 75cm (2½ft)
L. angustifolia 'Imperial Gem' – early, deep purple, stems are held upright for easy picking. H 60cm (2ft)

Lavandula × intermedia 'Grosso'

L. × intermedia 'Grosso' – the most commonly grown variety for oil production, with powerful scent, good for dried bunches. H 75cm (2½ft)

SPACING: 30–45cm (12–17½in) apart.

CULTIVATION TIPS: Cut back to 25cm (10in) immediately after flowering to ensure long stems the following year.

WHEN TO HARVEST: Once a third of the florets are open on a stem; at this stage they will remain on the stems when dried.

CONDITIONING AND VASE LIFE: If using a glass vase, change the water daily as it discolours very quickly; 10 days.

USES: I bunch a few stems together for more impact, working them into an arrangement as a group. To dry lavender, hang bunches in a dark, well-ventilated room for two weeks.

PROPAGATION: By semi-ripe cuttings in summer.

Leycesteria formosa
Himalyan honeysuckle

A large, arching shrub which quickly forms a thicket of tall, hollow stems rather like bamboo, in late summer it bear long, dangling, tassel-like racemes of dark red bracts, with small white flowers. These are followed by shiny purple-black berries which nestle in the persistent bracts. This is an excellent plant for wildlife, with nectar-rich flowers and berries that are enjoyed by birds. It is fast-growing, tolerant of any soil and happy in full sun or part shade. H 1.8m (6ft)

SPACING: 75cm (2½ft) apart.

CULTIVATION TIPS: Coppice annually to 15cm (6in) in early spring. Mulch and protect new growth from late frosts.

WHEN TO HARVEST: Stems can be cut from flowering through to fruiting, which is a harvest period of three months.

CONDITIONING AND VASE LIFE: Re-cut hollow stems under water; 14 days

USES: The long stems with their hanging flowers add height and drama to arrangements. I often remove some of the large leaves, which can be a little heavy.

PROPAGATION: By softwood cuttings in early summer.

Leycesteria formosa

Magnolia × *soulangeana*
Saucer magnolia

I always think of cutting magnolia branches with their flushed pink goblet-shaped flowers as rather decadent, since it feels like a real treat to bring a few branches into the house. Perhaps it is because they are such slow-growers, taking many years to mature into a small tree, or that they are only in their full flowering glory for a couple of weeks in early spring, sometimes less if a frost spoils their large waxen flowers. The most commonly grown and readily available magnolia, this one tolerates alkaline soil and is very hardy. It will do best in a sheltered position away from strong winds and in full sun. H 4m (13ft)

SPACING: 1.5m (5ft) apart.

WHEN TO HARVEST: Flowers bruise very easily, so harvest when they are safely cocooned in their velvety buds.

CONDITIONING AND VASE LIFE: Woody cut; 7 days

USES: To achieve a natural-style arrangement reminiscent of the tree, try to place branches so they are positioned in the same way as they were growing, with the flowers held upright.

PROPAGATION: Get a head start with a containerized plant.

Magnolia × *soulangeana*. The best time to pick the branches is as the flowers are just breaking from their velvety buds.

Malus
Crab apple

A generous trees to grow for cutting, the crab apple has two equally glorious seasons. In mid-spring the branches are covered in clouds of pink and white blossom, while fruits and foliage provide rich autumnal colour. Both the flowering and fruiting seasons are longer than that of culinary apples, and they also have the advantage of producing flowers and fruit from three years old. They are excellent for wildlife with abundant pollen followed by fruit that stays on the branch well into winter. H 3-4m (10-13ft)

RECOMMENDED PLANTS: There are numerous cultivars to choose from; look for ones with disease-resistance and small fruits, for easier use in arrangements.

Malus 'Evereste' – a widely available cultivar with fragrant blossom and rust orange fruits. H.2.5m (8¼ft)

M. sylvestris – for fast growth and plentiful blossom, this native crab apple often supplied as a hedging plant is a very good option. H 3m (10ft)

SPACING: For a hedge, plant 1m (3¼ft) apart with 3m (10ft) wide paths in between rows.

WHEN TO HARVEST: Harvest the blossom in the coloured bud stage.

CONDITIONING AND VASE LIFE: Flowers on cut branches begin to drop after three to four days.

USES: Flowering and fruiting branches are framework elements.

SOURCING: Source as bare root hedging plants in dormant season.

Left: *Malus* 'Rudolph' has smoky pink blossom accompanied by bronzed foliage.

Right: *Malus hupehensis* has cherry sized, deep red fruit in mid-autumn.

Philadelphus
Mock orange

A plant that epitomizes the romantic, English-country-garden style, with fragrant white flowers that are perfectly timed for early summer weddings. There is much variation in the power and sweetness of their scent, with the best evoking the heady aroma of their namesake. The abundant cup-shaped flowers are a crisp white; some are doubles, but I am drawn to the simplicity of the singles. They are backed by fresh green foliage, with the arching stems providing plenty of length for large arrangements. Mock orange are hardy, adaptable plants that will be more productive if they are pruned annually.

RECOMMENDED PLANTS:
P. 'Belle Etoile' – a popular, relatively compact and widely available variety with a heady neroli fragrance and single white flowers stained maroon at the centre. H 1.5m (5ft)
P. coronarius 'Aureus' – a golden-leaved form which I use for its lime-green spring foliage. H 1.8m (6ft)
P. 'Enchantment' – large, fragrant, semi-double flowers, a Great Dixter favourite. H 2m (6½ft)

SPACING: 1m (3¼ft) apart.

CULTIVATION TIPS: The flowers are formed on last year's wood, so prune back to young growth after flowering – ideally, this pruning is done when the stems are harvested. Mock orange can become unproductive; if so, cut everything back to 20cm (8in) in late winter to rejuvenate.

WHEN TO HARVEST: Just as the flowers start to open.

CONDITIONING AND VASE LIFE: The stems benefit from a 30-second sear. Double-flowered types last longer than singles; 7 days

USES: They certainly merit arranging on their own but also make a useful frame-work material for summer arrangements.

PROPAGATION: By softwood cuttings in early summer.

Philadelphus 'Belle Etoile'. The maroon colouring in the centre of the single flowers gives them more definition, making this cultivar a useful supporting flower for the soft shapes of garden roses.

Physocarpus opulifolius
Ninebark

One of the highest-yielding woody cuts we grow, this plant is capable of surviving just about any growing situation. It is fast-growing and can produce harvestable stems a year after planting. The scale and shape of its three-lobed leaves integrate easily into arrangements. Plant in full sun for the best leaf colour. H 2.4m (8ft)

RECOMMENDED PLANTS:
P. opulifolius 'Dart's Gold' – best used when the golden foliage is emerging in early spring. H 1.8m (6ft)
P. opulifolius 'Diabolo' – dark burgundy leaves, white flowers and red seed pods. H 2.5m (8¼ft)

SPACING: 1.2m(4ft) apart.

CULTIVATION TIPS: Remove some of the older wood in late winter to prevent the plant becoming too congested and to encourage new growth from the base. These stems will be thinner and very

Physocarpus opulifolius 'Diabolo', the flowering branches are best picked when in beige-pink bud.

straight in their first year. I prefer second-year branches, which have developed a bit more character, produce flowers and have riper foliage which can be used in the spring.

WHEN TO HARVEST: It offers multiple cuts from the young emerging foliage in early spring to the flowering branches in midsummer; pick when the flower buds are coloured but not open.

CONDITIONING AND VASE LIFE: Woody cut; 10–14 days.

USES: I mostly use the coloured foliage as a supporting element. *P.* 'Dart's Gold' makes the perfect partnership with narcissi and the dark leaves of *P.* 'Diablo' add earthy depth and contrast.

PROPAGATION: Softwood cuttings in midsummer or pot up rooted suckers in the autumn.

Pittosporum tenuifolium 'Trim's Hedger'
Pittosporum

This evergreen shrub with small, shiny leaves on wiry, branching dark stems is a very hardy and vigorous form with fairly large, roundish leaves. A staple for supporting foliage, it will thrive in any well-drained soil, but does need a sheltered position out of cold, drying winds. H 1.8m (6ft)

RECOMMENDED PLANTS:
P. 'Arundel Green' – a fast-growing cultivar with wavy leaves. H 1.8m (6ft)
P. tenuifolium 'Silver Queen' – variegated leaves in a soft green with cream edges. H 1.8m (6ft)

SPACING: 1m apart.

WHEN TO HARVEST: The best time to harvest is after midsummer when the leaves are mature and feel leathery.

CONDITIONING AND VASE LIFE: Woody cut; 2-4 weeks depending on the maturity of the foliage.

USES: A good base for bouquets and installation work because of the mid-green colour, small leaves and branching structure.

PROPAGATION: By semi hardwood cuttings in late summer.

Pittosporum tenuifolium 'Trim's Hedger'

Prunus cerasifera
Cherry plum

The earliest of the blossoming branches; when the garden is still in unrelenting shades of buff, dun and grey this joyful froth is so very welcome. The fragrant white delicate flowers appear in late winter on naked, dark, twiggy stems. They can be planted as a relatively fast-growing hedge, with harvestable stems after two years. Their flowers are a valuable pollen and nectar source for early pollinators. H 3m (10ft) with annual tip pruning.

RECOMMENDED PLANTS:
P. cerasifera 'Pissardii' – pale pink flowers followed by deep burgundy foliage and, with luck, plum-like fruits. H 3m (10ft)
P. spinosa – known as blackthorn, this produces white star-shaped flowers all along the length of its dark bare stems at the same time as *P. cerasifera*. In mid-autumn, branches can be harvested again, this time for the stylish, inky-blue sloe berries. This thorny native hedge is a tough, fast-growing windbreak with high wildlife value. H 3m (10ft)

SPACING: For a double, staggered hedge, plant at 60cm (2ft) apart.

WHEN TO HARVEST: Ideally in bud and force indoors.

CONDITIONING AND VASE LIFE: 10 days if cut in tight bud.

USES: Their sparse beauty is best appreciated as a simple, stand-alone arrangement, which I think reflects how they are outside in the bare late winter garden.

SOURCING: Source as bare-root hedging plants in dormant season.

Prunus cerasifera var. *pissardii nigra* has the palest pink single flowers.

Ribes sanguineum
Flowering currant

One of the first flowering branches in early spring, these upright, deciduous shrubs produce a mass of pendulous flowers in pinks, crimsons and whites. The stems have a distinctive currant fragrance and the roundly palmate leaves are a fresh apple green. It is not fussy but will produce the most flowers in full sun and moist soil. H 2m (6½ft)

RECOMMENDED PLANTS:
R. sanguineum 'Elkington White' – a class act with large clusters of white, tinged pink, flowers. H 1.8m (6ft)

Ribes sanguineum 'Elkington White'

R. sanguineum 'Pulborough Scarlet' – a robust cultivar with deep, crimson pink flowers. H 2.5m (8¼ft)

SPACING: 1m (3¼ft) apart.

CULTIVATION TIPS: Prune in early summer by cutting back the flowered branches to a strong bud at least halfway down the plant.

WHEN TO HARVEST: When the flowers at the top of the flower cluster begin to open.

CONDITIONING AND VASE LIFE: Woody cut and sear. 7 days.

USES: The branching stems make a good framework for spring bulbs. I particularly like to team 'Elkington White' with creamy white anemones.

PROPAGATION: By hardwood cuttings in late winter.

Rosa
Rose

I find garden roses the most irresistible of flowers for the sense of nostalgia they evoke, their delicious scents and the way they elevate an arrangement into something that feels luxurious. It is easy to get carried away or feel bewildered while selecting your favourites for cutting. I have a few criteria to narrow down the search. First is health and vigour; we do not spray our roses for pests and diseases, so they must be robust enough to fend for themselves. This also means they will cope well with intensive harvesting and hard pruning. Next is their ability to repeat-flower, with at least two good flushes that continue for a few weeks in early summer and autumn. Thirdly is fragrance, which is what makes a rose so special. Some cultivars are more weatherproof than others – the modern floribunda, shrub and hybrid teas cope better with rain and scorching sun.

To ensure plants will be productive, just lightly deadhead the flowers in their first year. This means they can put their energy into developing a strong root system which will ultimately yield more harvestable stems in subsequent years. Roses grown for cut-flower use are usually worn out after about eight years and will need to be replaced with plants in a new position to avoid rose replant disease.

Below left: A bucketful of roses in harmonious colours displaying the variation in flower shape between hybrid tea, shrub and floribunda types.

Below right: *Rosa* 'Port Sunlight', one of the best David Austin roses.

Opposite page: *Rosa* 'Sally Holmes', reminiscent of a dog rose and producing large, single flowers profusely throughout the summer.

RECOMMENDED PLANTS:

R. A WHITER SHADE OF PALE – a very pale pink with lots of flowers on each stem, classic hybrid tea shape but more delicate than most. The most weather-resistant of our roses. H 90cm (3ft)

R. CHANDOS BEAUTY – hybrid tea, a favourite for scent, health and stem length, with apricot-pink, medium-sized flowers. It grows very tall, so is prone to wind rock. H 90cm (3ft)

R. DUCHESS OF CORNWALL – one of the Nostalgic series, with coral flowers reminiscent of an old rose but with much better disease-resistance and vase life. H 75cm (2½ft)

R. HOT CHOCOLATE – floribunda, with uniquely coloured clusters of flowers, orange buds opening to a velvety, rusty red-brown. Very prickly. H 1m (3¼ft).

R. IRISH HOPE – floribunda, pale lemon-coloured rose, very floriferous with generous trusses of cupped blooms that open into broad rosettes full of petals. Good vase life. H 1.2m (4ft)

R. 'Just Joey' – hybrid tea, large, loose, blowsy blooms in coppery orange. H 90cm (3ft)

R. PORT SUNLIGHT – shrub, David Austin rose, rich apricot-coloured medium-sized rosette-shaped flowers, thornless, with dark red stems. Very healthy with good repeat flowering. H 1.4m (4½ft)

R. PROPER JOB – one of the Nostalgic series, with rich burgundy-red, quartered flowers. H 1.2m (4ft)

R. 'Sally Holmes' – shrub, large arching trusses of of creamy-white single flowers, peach in bud, flowers continuously. Vigorous, needs space. H 1.5m (5ft)

R. STEPHEN RULO – hybrid tea, a real chameleon, this novel rose which you will either love or hate moves in colour from a milky coffee through to lavender grey. Healthy and productive. H 1m (3¼ft)

SPACING: 70cm (2¼ft) apart

CULTIVATION TIPS: Prune all types hard in late winter, down to 30–40cm (12–15½in) and mulch generously with well-rotted manure. This will promote strong, straight regrowth with enough stem length to cut. To keep the plants healthy and productive they must be fed regularly, initially with a specialist foliar feed for roses which is high in potassium followed by a weekly high-potash feed once they begin to flower. Deadhead each week and water well if dry. Lightly prune in the autumn, taking about one-third off the plants to prevent wind rock.

WHEN TO HARVEST: Just as the outer petals are starting to unfurl and they look about a third of the way open.

CONDITIONING AND VASE LIFE: Sear; 3-7 days. Vase life depends on the variety – the more fragrant the rose the shorter the vase life.

USES: I like to combine two or three varieties in contrasting forms but similar colours. For a garden-to-vase look I select stems at different stages of growth – some blowsy and full-blown, others unscrolling from their buds.

PROPAGATION: Buy as bare-root plants in the dormant season, they are cheaper and with a larger root system which will establish more readily.

ROSE KEY

1. *R.* 'Natasha Richardson'
2. *R.* CARAMEL ANTIKE
3. *R.* 'Jude the Obscure'
4. *R.* ROMANTIC ANTIKE
5. *R.* 'Chandos Beauty'
6. *R.* 'Duchess of Cornwall'
7. *R.* 'Koko Loko'
8. *R.* 'Sally Holmes'
9. *R.* 'A Whiter Shade of Pale'
10. *R.* 'Moody Blue'
11. *R.* 'Margaret Merril'
12. *R.* 'Port Sunlight'
13. *R.* 'Stephen Rulo'
14. *R.* 'Queen of Sweden'
15. *R.* 'Golden Celebration'
16. *R.* 'Champagne Moment'
17. *R.* 'Sweet Child of Mine'
18. *R.* 'Hot Chocolate'
19. *R.* 'Just Joey'
20. *R.* 'Chris Beardshaw'

Left: *Rosa* 'Duchess of Cornwall' in all its shades of apricot-pink and deep coral.

Rosa glauca
RED-LEAVED ROSE

One of my must-have shrubs for foliage. I love the unique plum-grey colour of its leaves which are not as harsh as many purple-leaved shrubs and seem to compliment anything they are arranged with. The flowers are unremarkable and do not make an appearance if it is pruned annually for richer foliage colour. Full sun will bring out more coppery tints. Thankfully the graceful, arching stems are blessed with few thorns. This tough species rose is a good candidate as part of a cutting hedge. It is fast growing so will quickly provide cutting material and shelter. H 1.5m (5ft)

SPACING: 1m (3¼ft) with annual pruning

CULTIVATION TIPS: Prune to 30cm (1ft) in late winter and apply a generous mulch of compost.

WHEN TO HARVEST: Harvest after midsummer when the stems have ripened and the leaves feel slightly leathery.

CONDITIONING AND VASE LIFE: Woody cut and remove thorns.

USES: The serpentine stems are a gift for creating loose, asymmetrical displays. The earthy colour adds depth and effortless style.

PROPAGATION: By hardwood cuttings in the autumn or buy as bare root hedging plants.

Rosa glauca is at its best after midsummer when the foliage has ripened but still has a good depth of colour.

Rosmarinus officinalis
Rosemary

This well-known strongly aromatic herb is an evergreen shrub which we harvest regularly from midsummer through to early spring. The species form is a good one to start with; it is a deep emerald green and has a bushy habit. H 1.2m (4ft)

RECOMMENDED PLANTS: *Rosmarinus officinalis* 'Miss Jessopp's Upright' – as the name suggests, this cultivar has vigorous, upright growth and is one of the most frost-hardy. The needle-like leaves are finer than the species and more of a grey-green. H 1.2m (4ft)

SPACING: 45cm (17½in) apart

CULTIVATION TIPS: Prune in early spring by cutting back the plant by a third, avoiding going into non-productive wood. This will prolong the life of the plant and produce vigorous fresh growth to harvest once it is ripe. When to

Rosmarinus officinalis 'Miss Jessopp's Upright' has very fine needle-like foliage in an olive-green.

harvest: Wait until the tips have ripened, by midsummer.

CONDITIONING AND VASE LIFE: The cut stems turn water brown very quickly, so avoid using a glass vase and change the water frequently. 14 days.

USES: It is the most requested plant I grow for its meaning, as it signifies love and remembrance. It holds well out of water once it is ripe.

PROPAGATION: By semi-ripe cuttings in late summer.

Rubus idaeus 'All Gold'
Raspberry 'All Gold'

An autumn-fruiting raspberry bearing large, soft golden fruits. The berries blend well with other colours and are large enough not to be overshadowed by the leaves. Autumn-fruiting raspberries are a fast-growing source of both foliage and fruiting stems. They are self-supporting so require very little maintenance and have a long fruiting period from late summer to mid-autumn. H 1.5m (5ft)

RECOMMENDED PLANTS: *R. idaeus* 'Autumn Treasure' – a red-fruited, spine-free variety. H 1.2m (4ft)

SPACING: 45cm (17½in) for fruiting branches but can be closer if you are harvesting the stems for foliage.

CULTIVATION TIPS: Prune back all the canes to the ground in late winter.

Rubus idaeus 'All Gold' begins to bear fruit in late summer and is still productive by late autumn.

WHEN TO HARVEST: The attractive textural foliage can be cut earlier in the season and will shoot again, producing further cuts. Wait for the berries until they show colour but feel firm.

CONDITIONING AND VASE LIFE: 10 days.

USES: The glowing fruits impart a feeling of lushness reminiscent of a Dutch master painting. They make a strong textural accent, linking seasonal focal flowers to the first flush of autumnal colour in foliage.

PROPAGATION: We rotate our raspberries every 7 years. Lift canes in the dormant season with as much root as possible and plant in a new area.

Salix
Pussy willow

Pussy willow is one of the first plants I venture into the garden to pick each year. The soft, silvery-grey catkins appear on long, dark, slender stems in late winter and are one of earliest signs that spring is on its way. Willows are notoriously vigorous and can easily put on a couple of metres of growth in one year, which makes them an ideal candidate for a wind-breaking cutting hedge.

RECOMMENDED PLANTS: By selecting a few different varieties you can extend the season and have a range of catkins in different colours and shapes from late winter to early spring.
Salix gracilistyla – my staple species, as it is the earliest and most productive. The stems dry well, so I can use it for a few months after harvesting. The large, plump catkins measuring 2.5cm (1in) long have a warm rosy glow. H 3m (10ft)
S. gracilistyla 'Mount Aso' – developed in Japan, this has eye-catching rosy-pink catkins. H 1.5m (5ft)
S. purpurea 'Nancy Saunders' – the wiry mahogany stems are clothed in myriad tiny grey catkins. I pick this one year-round for its delicate grey-green foliage. H 2m (6½ft)

SPACING: 1m (3¼ft) apart.

CULTIVATION TIPS: Regular pruning is necessary to keep the catkins evenly spaced on the stems and within reach of a pair of secateurs. Our crop is divided into two, which get pollarded alternately every other year. Where the plants are cut will determine the size of the future stems – I take ours back to about 60cm (2ft), which yields medium-length stems. This is best done immediately after flowering once the catkins drop off.

WHEN TO HARVEST: As catkins begin to elongate and have a good silvery, almost metallic, sheen. If they have started to bloom and show a good deal of yellow pollen it is too late, but on the upside they will offer early pollen for the bees.

CONDITIONING AND VASE LIFE: If placed in water they will continue to open and flower, so I tend to dry mine out first. To dry, place the stems in empty buckets somewhere cool and dark. They will then last about a month before the catkins start to drop.

USES: The catkin branches add framework and texture to spring-flowering bulbs.

PROPAGATION: By hardwood cuttings after leaf fall. Cut stems into 45cm (17½in) lengths and push 15cm (6in) into the ground. The success rate will be higher if membrane is used to reduce weed competition.

Sarcococca hookeriana var. digyna
Sweet box

A compact, thicket-forming evergreen shrub with slender, glossy, rich green leaves. In late winter, small white spidery flowers appear along the stems; this is when the real value of this plant is revealed as you catch a waft of its heady perfume. It reminds me of honey and a little goes a long way in a room. It is a valuable plant for a sheltered, shadier area where it will quietly get on with things without any maintenance. It is slow-growing so harvest judiciously. H 1.2m (4ft)

SPACING: 50cm (19½in) apart.

WHEN TO HARVEST: When the flowers are fresh and white.

CONDITIONING AND VASE LIFE: Woody cut; 14 days.

USES: Adds perfume and is a good deep green supporting foliage to hellebores, snowdrops and pussy willow.

PROPAGATION: Pot on rooted suckers.

Sarcococca hookeriana var. *digyna* growing in a north-facing border where it enjoys the shade and shelter.

Sorbus aria
Whitebeam

The colour of this deciduous tree's foliage when it first unfolds is the softest pistachio green. I have not yet discovered another woody cut that comes close to its unique colour. The fact that it only stays like this for a few weeks before deepening to a grey-green makes it even more special. When the new downy leaves unfurl they resemble magnolia flowers with small bunches of embryonic white flowers at their centres. It is a slow-growing, medium-sized tree, domed and compact in shape. If you are impatient this is definitely a good foraging candidate as it will take about ten years before it is mature enough to harvest.

SPACING: 2m (6½ft) apart.

WHEN TO HARVEST: At the budding branch stage in mid-spring.

CONDITIONING AND VASE LIFE: Woody cut; 7 days.

USES: As a framework plant with leaves of a gentle colour that perfectly compliments pastel-coloured varieties of ranunculus and tulips.

PROPAGATION: Buy as a bare root sapling.

The soft green foliage is perfectly timed to accompany apple blossom and the ice cream shades of pastel ranunculus.

Spiraea thunbergii
Thunberg spiraea

This is one of our earliest-flowering shrubs, coming into bloom just as the cherry plum and blackthorn are fading. Its wispy branches awaken with a peppering of small, delicate white flowers and slender fresh-green leaves, taking up the mantle of supporting flower for all the spring-flowering bulbs that we are beginning to harvest. It is very hardy and will tolerate an exposed site; position it in full sun or partial shade. H 1m (3¼ft)

RECOMMENDED PLANTS: S. 'Arguta' – the taller, rangier bridal wreath begins to flower as *S. thunbergii* finishes in mid-spring, offering a seamless continuity of flowering branches for spring displays. The slender, arching stems are covered in a profusion of tiny white flowers. It is easy and productive. H 1m (3¼ft)

SPACING: 1m (3¼ft) apart.

CULTIVATION TIPS: Prune out old and unproductive stems after flowering to encourage vigorous regrowth and more stems to cut the following season.

WHEN TO HARVEST: Spiraea has three valued stages of harvest: first the flowering branches in early spring, then for its feathery fronds of bright green foliage through the summer and finally its burnished autumn colour, with leaves that hold on well to their stems once cut. To make these multiple cuts I recommend growing at least twice as much as you think you will need.

CONDITIONING AND VASE LIFE: Cut when a third of the flowers on the stem are open. Woody cut; 7–14 days.

USES: The blossoming branches have a lax habit which softens the upright stems of spring-flowering bulbs. It has become a favourite foliage during the summer for its shape and lightness of touch in bouquets. By autumn it becomes more of an accent plant as its leaves thin out, exposing the finest of stems and brushes of colour that weave beautifully through chrysanthemums and dahlias.

PROPAGATION: By softwood cuttings in early summer.

Top left: *Spiraea thunbergii* displaying feathery brushstrokes of autumnal colour.

Top right: *Spiraea* 'Arguta' in full flower in mid-spring.

Right: *Spiraea thunbergii* with a peppering of dainty flowers in early spring.

Symphoricarpos hybrids
Snowberry

I discovered these berried shrubs through a Dutch nursery called Kolster, which has developed a number of hybrids specifically for the cut-flower trade called the Magical series. If you think of snowberries as a scruffy, suckering thicket with a few sparse berries to be had, these are in another league. They have the characteristic pearly berries in hues of pink, purple, white and green which are borne on upright, thin stems which are easy to harvest. The plants form well-behaved clumps and the berries are so abundant that many of the stems take on a pleasing arching form. The small pink flowers are a favourite with the honey bees. They are easy-to-grow, adaptable plants and my most regularly harvested and arranged fruiting stems. H 1m (3¼ft)

RECOMMENDED PLANTS:
MAGICAL AUTUMN BLUSH – blush pink and at its best in mid-autumn. H 1m (3¼ft)
MAGICAL CHARMING FANTASY – pink with a long harvest period from late summer to mid-autumn. H 1m (3¼ft)
MAGICAL MAGNIFICENCE – white with a taller more upright habit, can be harvested to late autumn. H 1.2m (4ft)

SPACING: 80cm (2¾ft) apart.

CULTIVATION TIPS: The flowers and fruits are produced on first-year wood, so cut back hard in late winter.

WHEN TO HARVEST: The youngest fruits on the stem should still be immature.

CONDITIONING AND VASE LIFE: Woody cut; 10 days

USES: I also harvest snowberry for its foliage, before the berries have formed.

The small rounded leaves are blue-green on well-branched woody stems. The fruiting stems are a staple supporting material for roses and dahlias.

PROPAGATION: Softwood cuttings in early summer root easily.

Symphoricarpos MAGICAL AUTUMN BLUSH

Syringa vulgaris
Lilac

Foraging for lilac on the farm has become an annual ritual. Just a five-minute walk from G&G HQ there is an ancient hedge of it and in late spring it becomes a billowing mass of richly fragrant flowers in pinks, mauves and whites, stretching off into the distance. Its flowering period is a glorious but fleeting two weeks but is perfectly timed for a rather tricky in-between stage in the garden. Lilacs are slow to mature, taking at least four years before they produce their first flowers. I can forgive the wait for their minimal maintenance and hardy nature. They enjoy fertile, well-drained soil in full sun and thrive on chalk. H 2.5m (8¼ft)

RECOMMENDED PLANTS: I prefer the single-flowered cultivars and tend to go for those of *S. vulgaris* as they suit our climate and tend to be very fragrant, particularly the paler varieties.

SPACING: 1.2m (4ft) apart.

CULTIVATION TIPS: Deadhead after flowering. On older plants, remove one-third of older wood every year during the dormant season. It is also sensible to control the height so that you can reach the flowering stems.

WHEN TO HARVEST: Pick when three-quarters of the flower panicle is open, as they will not develop from tight buds. Do not be afraid to harvest a decent length of stem, as it encourages strong, long regrowth the following year.

CONDITIONING AND VASE LIFE: Woody cut and condition in a deep bucket of warm water overnight; to prolong vase life to five days, remove all the leaves except the ones immediately below the flowers.

USES: Lilac is beautiful arranged on its own or as a supporting flower with spring-flowering bulbs.

PROPAGATION: From rooted suckers produced at the base of the plant or if you want particular cultivars buy as containerized plants.

Syringa vulgaris, one of my favourite flowering branches to arrange on its own.

Viburnum opulus
Guelder rose

This species forms a valuable part of our cutting hedge, as it is a tough, adaptable British native able to grow on most soils in full sun or partial shade. Guelder rose flowers late spring to early summer with berries in autumn offering pollen and fruit for wildlife and multiple stages of harvest. It is vigorous, putting on up to 40cm of growth a year, and does not mind being picked after three years. It can happily reach 3m (10ft) in height but with regular harvesting of the leading stems will be kept in check.

RECOMMENDED PLANTS: 'Roseum' has pompom-shaped flowers which turn from apple-green to creamy snowballs over a period of about two weeks. It is sterile, so is not followed by berries, but it comes into flower two weeks before the species. By growing both you can competently fill the interlude between spring and summer. H 3m (10ft)

SPACING: 1m (3¼ft) apart.

CULTIVATION TIPS: Prune established plants immediately after flowering, removing a third of the older wood.

WHEN TO HARVEST: Late spring white flowers resembling small lacecap hydrangea are followed by red fruits in autumn. I prefer to harvest the berries in late summer when they are just starting to turn from yellow to red, as at this stage they are two-toned and far more interesting.

CONDITIONING AND VASE LIFE: Woody cut and sear for 30 seconds, then plunge them into deep cool water to drink overnight. 7 days.

USES: The creamy-green flowers make great supporting flowers and foliage for spring flowering bulbs.

PROPAGATION: By softwood cuttings or layering.

Clockwise from top left: berries in late summer at the two-tone stage; lacecap flowers in late spring; hedge of *Viburnum opulus* 'Roseum'.

Weigela
Weigela

I grow weigela primarily for its foliage which is fast growing, upright and available in a good range of colours. The tubular flowers produced in midsummer are not my favourite shades of pinks and reds, plus there are plenty of other things to choose from at that time of year. It is an easy to grow, adaptable plant which produces a lot of material after just two years.

Weigela florida 'Variegata', produces very straight stems which are useful for bouquet work.

RECOMMENDED PLANTS:
W. florida 'Variegata' is a smart ivory and green combination which takes on coppery-pink tints in the autumn.
W. 'Briant Rubidor' bright golden foliage that keeps its colour if harvested regularly.

HEIGHT AND SPACING: 1.5m by 1m (5ft x 3¼ft)

CULTIVATION TIPS: For foliage cut back to 60cm (2ft) in late winter.

WHEN TO HARVEST: Cut when the stems ripen in late summer to leaf fall.

CONDITIONING AND VASE LIFE:
Woody cut. 14 days

USES: I wait until the foliage has some coppery autumn colour, then it combines well with chrysanthemums and grasses. The straight stems are useful for bouquet work.

PROPAGATION: By softwood cuttings in early summer.

Recommended Suppliers

BULBS AND PERENNIALS

Arvensis Perennials
www.arvensisperennials.co.uk
A trade-only nursery specializing in herbaceous perennials and grasses, with a focus on plants that create a naturalistic style.

Howards Nurseries Ltd
www.howardnurseries.co.uk
A large wholesale perennial specialist nurseries, with an excellent mail order service and plenty of open-ground stock including irises and peonies.

Peter Nyssen
www.peternyssen.com
A wide selection of spring- and autumn-planted bulbs, which are not treated with neonicotinoids. Large orders are at a discounted price.

Rare Plant Fair
www.rareplantfair.co.uk
Fairs held throughout the growing season across the South and South West of England, South Wales and the West Midlands.

Rose Cottage Plants
www.rosecottageplants.co.uk
A nursery that is always up with the latest trends in colour and form, selling hardy perennials and bulbs.

Wildegoose Nursery and Garden
www.wildegoosenursery.co.uk
Specialist growers of hardy perennials, with inspiring display borders in a beautiful walled garden setting.

SHRUBS

Kolster
www.kolster.nl
Dutch specialists in breeding shrubs for cutting; their Magical ranges of hypericum and snowberry are particularly good.

CHRYSANTHEMUMS

Deconova
www.deconova.eu
The largest range of single-headed bloom chrysanthemums, available as rooted cuttings in units of one hundred, ordered through a representative.

CLEMATIS

Taylors Clematis
www.taylorsclematis.co.uk
A good range of herbaceous clematis recommended for cut flower use.

DAHLIAS

Halls of Heddon
www.hallsofheddon.co.uk
A company with 100 years' experience of growing dahlias – a good place to buy rooted cuttings and pot tubers, healthy and virus-free stock.

EUCALYPTUS

Grafton Nursery
www.hardy-eucalyptus.com
The leading supplier of eucalyptus to cut-foliage growers in the UK, with well-grown trees and good advice on choosing the right species for your site.

ORNAMENTAL GRASSES

Knoll Gardens
www.knollgardens.co.uk
A 1.6 hectare (4 acre) display garden is by the nursery.

PEONIES

Comptoir Paulinois
www.comptoir_paulinois.com
For larger quantities of bare-root peonies.

ROSES

Pococks Roses
www.garden-roses.co.uk
Field-grown bare-root roses of exceptional quality.

SEED

Chiltern Seeds
www.chilternseeds.co.uk
A wide range of ornamental and vegetable seeds.

Green and Gorgeous
www.greenandgorgeousflowers.co.uk
Much of our cut-flower seed collection is perennial and very fresh because it is saved from what we grow.

Jelitto
www.jelitto.com
A huge selection of perennial seeds, excellent germination, detailed sowing instructions and recommended species and cultivars for cutting.

SPECIAL PLANTS
www.specialplants.net
Self-confessed plantaholic Derry Watkins has a fabulous nursery and online seed catalogue with lots of unusual treasures.

TOOLS
Niwaki
www.niwaki.com
A one-stop shop for hand tools, including the best selection of snips and secateurs for harvesting.

GREENHOUSES
www.kedergreenhouse.co.uk

VASES
Some of my vases are sourced from local antique and bric-a-brac shops, some made by myself or by local potters. A number of the vases in this book are made by Harriet Coleridge, with whom I have collaborated over the years. She has four kilns to create different surfaces to her masterfully thrown pots.
www.harrietcoleridge.co.uk

Further Reading

This book is intended to inspire and encourage a garden-led approach to growing and arranging flowers. I wrote it because I felt it was time that the perennials and woody plants, which many of us grow in our gardens, were championed for their sustainable and creative credentials as cut flowers and foliage. The books that follow are some of my staple references that expand upon the topics and material I have covered.

Designing with Plants by Piet Oudolf with Noel Kingsbury. Published in 1999 by Conrad Octopus Limited. A useful book for translating the philosophy of naturalistic garden design to the vase.

Floret Farm's Discovering Dahlias: A Guide to Growing and Arranging Magnificent Blooms by Erin Benzakein. Published in 2021 by Chronicle Books. From the queen of flower farmers, a beautifully photographed deep delve into growing and arranging with dahlias.

Garden to Vase: Growing and using your own cut flowers by Linda Beutler. Published by Timber Press in 2007. A useful directory of 200 plants many of which are perennials and shrubs.

Fantastic Foliage and how to Farm It: The essential guide to growing cut Eucalyptus by Hilary Collins. Published in 2019. A detailed guide to variety selection and maintenance of eucalyptus to ensure an ongoing healthy supply of foliage from year to year.

Late Summer Flowers by Marina Christopher. Published by Frances Lincoln in 2006. An impeccable selection of later flowering perennials with some good practical advice on propagation.

The Cutting Garden: Growing and Arranging Garden Flowers by Sarah Raven. Published by Frances Lincoln in 1996. My first book on growing cut flowers and still one of the best, particularly for its plant directory which is organised by season and colour and includes many perennials and shrubs.

The Propagation of Hardy Perennials by Richard Bird. Published by B.T. Batsford Ltd in 1993. An A-Z guide of plants by genus and in some cases species if there is any variation in propagation methods.

Woody Cut Stems for Growers and Florists: Production and Post-Harvest Handling of Branches for Flowers, Fruit and Foliage by Lane Greer and John M.Dole. Published by Timber Press in 2008. An in-depth guide which excels in information on plant spacing and pruning.

Index

Page numbers in *italic* type refer to pictures.